Dealing with Emotional Problems in Coaching

I0121827

This book is a comprehensive guide for coaches on how to use rational-emotive and cognitive behaviour therapy (RECBT) to help coachees with their emotional problems within a coaching context. In this fully updated new edition, Windy Dryden:

- discusses the eight major emotions that feature in coachees' emotional problems and their healthy alternatives
- outlines a step-by-step guide to the use of RECBT in the coaching context
- illustrates these points with a case of a coachee whose progress towards a personal development objective was hampered by an emotional problem and how the coach implemented RECBT to help her deal with the obstacle and resume development-based coaching.

Dealing with Emotional Problems in Coaching will be a valuable resource for all those involved in coaching.

Windy Dryden, PhD, is Emeritus Professor of Psychotherapeutic Studies at Goldsmiths, University of London, and is an international authority on rational emotive behaviour therapy (REBT). He has worked in psychotherapy for over 45 years and is the author and editor of over 230 books.

Dealing with Emotional Problems in Coaching

A Rational-Emotive and Cognitive-Behavioural Approach

Second Edition

Windy Dryden

Routledge
Taylor & Francis Group

LONDON AND NEW YORK

Second edition published 2021
by Routledge
2 Park Square, Milton Park, Abingdon, Oxon OX14 4RN

and by Routledge
52 Vanderbilt Avenue, New York, NY 10017

Routledge is an imprint of the Taylor & Francis Group, an informa business

First edition published 2011 by Routledge

British Library Cataloguing-in-Publication Data
A catalogue record for this book is available from the British Library

Library of Congress Cataloging-in-Publication Data
Names: Dryden, Windy, author.
Title: Dealing with emotional problems in coaching : a rational-emotive
and cognitive-behavioural approach / Windy Dryden.
Other titles: Dealing with clients' emotional problems in life coaching
Identifiers: LCCN 2020026227 (print) | LCCN 2020026228 (ebook) |
ISBN 9780367556204 (hardback) | ISBN 9780367556211 (paperback) |
ISBN 9781003094340 (ebook)
Subjects: LCSH: Personal coaching. | Rational emotive behavior therapy.
Classification: LCC BF637.P36 D79 2021 (print) |
LCC BF637.P36 (ebook) | DDC 158.3–dc23
LC record available at https://lccn.loc.gov/2020026227
LC ebook record available at https://lccn.loc.gov/2020026228

ISBN: 9780367556204 (hbk)
ISBN: 9780367556211 (pbk)
ISBN: 9781003094340 (ebk)

Typeset in Sabon
by Newgen Publishing UK

Contents

Introduction

Coaching is a practice designed to help coachees to identify and achieve their personal development objectives. It is generally a present-centred and future-focused way of working where coach and coachee work together in a collaborative way in the pursuit of the coachee's objectives. While coaches distinguish themselves from therapists (particularly those who help people deal with conflicts rooted in the past), there are times in coaching where the coachee gets stuck because she (in this case) experiences an emotional problem that is not easily resolved by the coach's standard interventions.

As such, if you, as a coach, are going to offer your coachees a comprehensive service, it is important that (1) you have a working knowledge of common emotional problems that serve as obstacles to the achievement of coachee personal development objectives; (2) you understand what constitutes healthy alternatives to these emotional problems; and (3) you have a framework for helping your coachees to deal with these emotional problems in a constructive way so that they can get on with the business of working towards realising their personal development objectives. The aim of this book is to cover these three points.

Having said this, it is useful to remember that your basic goal as a coach is to help your coachee to identify, pursue and ultimately achieve her personal development objectives and not to help her with her emotional problems *per se*. The position that I take in this book is that you should deal with your coachee's emotional problem if you are trained to do so. If not, you should refer them to a professional who has such training.

I have three goals in writing this book. First, I will outline the central role played by attitudes in explaining your coachees' disturbed and constructive responses to adversities. Second, I will provide you with a working knowledge of common emotional problems that you are likely to encounter in the course of your career as a coach and an understanding of what constitutes healthy alternatives to these emotional problems. Third, I present a step-by-step guide to dealing with your coachees' emotional problems when these problems explain why your coachees become stuck in the coaching process. This guide is based on the insights of a therapeutic tradition known as cognitive behaviour therapy (CBT) and particularly on the ideas of Dr Albert Ellis (1913–2007), the founder of rational emotive behaviour therapy, a distinctive approach within the CBT tradition. When referring to the approach that underpins this book, I will speak of rational-emotive and cognitive behaviour therapy (RECBT).

This book is best considered as a companion rather than a training course. If you wish to train in RECBT, please refer to www.albertellisinstitute.org or www.arebt.one for relevant information.

Why deal with problematic emotions in coaching?

In my experience using RECBT as a coach and counsellor, I have found that coachees present with one or more of eight common emotional problems that, when coachees cannot deal with them on their own, serve as major obstacles to them pursuing their personal development objectives. These are: anxiety, depression, shame, guilt, hurt, problematic anger, problematic jealousy and problematic envy. As you will presently see, coachees experience these problematic emotions when they encounter life's adversities. Although you may be tempted as a coach to bypass these problematic emotions and help your coachees, in the first instance, to change these adversities, you will find that if you take this stance it will not be terribly effective. This is because problematic emotions, if not dealt with, will usually have a negative impact on your coachees' attempts to change these adversities. So, in RECBT, we argue that, most of the time, the most effective long-term strategy in dealing with the presence of coachees' emotional problems is to help your coachees to address them before encouraging them to change the adversities about which they have the emotional problem, if, indeed, the adversities can be changed. If the adversities cannot be changed, then the fact that you have helped your coachees to deal with their emotional problems means that they will be better placed to move on with achieving their personal development objectives than if their emotional problems were in place.

However, it is important to stress that in RECBT not all negative emotions are considered problematic and serve as obstacles to the pursuit of personal development objectives. Some negative emotions represent constructive responses to life's adversities and help people both to process what has happened to them and to deal with the adversities as productively as they can before either resuming the pursuit of their personal development objectives or setting new goals. An understanding of what underlies these problematic and constructive negative emotions is crucial if you are to use RECBT constructively in the course of your coaching practice and I begin the book, in Part 1, with a presentation of RECBT's position on this point. But first a word of caution about the step-by-step guide presented in Part 3.

When to deal with emotional problems in coaching

When I present on dealing with emotional problems in coaching, perhaps the most frequent question I am asked concerns *when* a coach should do so. From the point of view of this book, the answer is clear. Deal with an emotional problem if it emerges as an obstacle to the work you are doing to help the person reach their personal development objectives and you are trained to do so. However, people also seek the help of coaches for their emotional problems rather than to set and pursue personal development objectives since approaching a coach for help with such problems is more acceptable to them than approaching a therapist or counsellor.

If this applies to you, then my advice is to help the person with their emotional problem if you are trained and competent to do so, perhaps using this book as a framework. However, my advice is also to bear in mind a set of criteria put forward by Michael Cavanagh (2005), an Australian coaching psychologist, concerning when coaches should help coachees with their emotional problems and when they should not.

Cavanagh's (2005) criteria

Cavanagh (2005), in an important chapter on mental health issues in executive coaching, outlined several guidelines to help coaches decide whether to offer coaching to executives in distress. I use his guidelines to answer coaches' questions concerning whether or not to offer to help a person who has sought coaching help for an emotional problem.

1. *How long has the person been experiencing the emotional problem?*
   If the emotional problem is of recent origin or if it occurs intermittently, then coaching for the emotional problem may be considered. However, if it occurs persistently or is chronic, then such coaching is not indicated and a judicious referral to a counsellor or psychotherapist or other mental-health specialist may be required.

2. *How extreme are the responses of the applicant?*

    If the person's emotional, behavioural and/or thinking responses to the relevant adversity are distressing to the person but lie within a mild to moderate range of distress, then coaching for the emotional problem may be considered. However, if the applicant's distress is extreme, then such coaching is probably not indicated.

3. *How pervasive is the emotional problem?*

    If the person's emotional problem is limited to a certain situation or aspect of the person's life, then coaching for the emotional problem may be considered. However, if it occurs in many situations and on many occasions, then such coaching again is probably not indicated.

4. *How defensive is the person with respect to their emotional problem?*

    The person may meet the above three criteria with respect to the emotional problem for which they are seeking help, but still not be suitable for coaching because of their high level of defensiveness with respect to the problem. Signs of this include: a) actively seeking to avoid addressing the problem; b) being told that they have to seek help by someone and denying they have the problem themself; c) showing in their responses that they would struggle to cooperate with the coach when addressing the problem. Again a judicious referral to a mental-health specialist better trained and more experienced to deal with such defensiveness is in order.

5. *How resistant to change is the emotional problem?*

    If it appears that the emotional problem is likely to persist despite the person's apparent willingness to address it, then this may indicate that the person is likely to have great difficulty in addressing the problem. While this can only really be judged once the coach and the person have decided to work together to address the problem in coaching, if the person has failed to address the problem several times before in different ways, then this may be a contraindication for coaching.

My advice here would be this. If the person's emotional problem is intermittent, non-pervasive, non-extreme and they indicate they can cooperate with you, then if their problem has seemed resistant to change in the past, offer to take them on if you can offer a fresh approach to the problem and one that makes sense to them and they will agree to be referred to someone with more experience at dealing with the emotional problem than you if the problem continues to be resistant to change.

Why RECBT is suited to dealing with emotional problems in coaching

RECBT is, in some respects, ideally suited to dealing with emotional problems in the practice of coaching for a number of reasons.

- It enables you to engage your coachee quickly in the process of identifying and dealing with her emotional problem.
- It encourages you to be explicit with your coachee concerning what you plan to do and encourages her to give her informed consent.
- It helps your coachee to stay focused.
- It encourages your coachee to be as specific as possible.
- It urges you to interrupt your coachee when appropriate, but do so with tact.
- It alerts you to the importance of making sure that your coachee answers the questions you ask her.
- It encourages you to give your coachee time to answer your questions.
- It stresses the importance of helping your coachee to identify and respond to your coachee's doubts, reservations

and objections, including those that may be expressed non-verbally.

- It urges you to check out your coachee's understanding of your substantive points.

The step-by-step guide: a word of caution

If you know anything about jazz, you will know that before you can skilfully improvise on your chosen instrument, you will need to play it properly. This requires you to play and learn musical scales and chords. When you have done this, your improvisation will be based on a sound foundation. The same is true when learning how to practise RECBT well. The steps I will present in this step-by-step guide represent roughly the order that you need to practise them with your coachees and you need to learn this sequence before you can improvise with deftness and skill. Once you have done so, avoid using the steps stiltedly and in an overly formalised way, although you will tend to practise RECBT in this way while you are learning the steps. In a nutshell, you need to avoid two errors:

- Do not improvise until you have learned how to use the steps in the guide.
- Do not be overly formal and stilted in your use of the steps when you are ready to improvise.

Windy Dryden, April 2020   London and Eastbourne

Part I

The central role played by attitudes in understanding your coachees' problematic and constructive negative emotions

RECBT theory is based on an old dictum attributed to the Stoic philosopher Epictetus which can be summed up in the phrase: people are disturbed not by things, but by their views of things. This clearly shows the importance of cognitive factors in emotional problems. Albert Ellis, the founder of rational emotive behaviour therapy, developed this point to help us distinguish between negative emotions that are problematic and those that are constructive. Ellis's position can be summarised as follows.

- People experience problematic negative emotions about life's adversities when they hold rigid and extreme attitudes[1] towards these adversities.
- People experience constructive negative emotions about life's adversities when they hold flexible and non-extreme attitudes towards these adversities.

As you can see from the above, RECBT's view is that the attitudes that we hold towards the adversities that we face are central to the way we respond emotionally to these adversities. In addition, these attitudes also determine how we respond behaviourally to these adversities and how we subsequently think about them, as we will presently see.

In order to help your coachees deal with the emotionally based obstacles to their personal development objectives, it is important that you understand the role that attitudes play in emotional disturbance and in emotional health. I will begin by outlining the attitudes that underpin emotional disturbance that are rigid and extreme in nature.

Understanding rigid and extreme attitudes

In explaining the role that rigid and extreme attitudes play in your coachees' emotional problems, I will illustrate my points by discussing the case of Linda who sought coaching because she was not being challenged in life. I helped her to set a number of goals that she prioritised and then began to take action on. Soon after, she failed to get a promotion at work that she had been promised by her boss. This adversity constituted a potential obstacle to her working towards her personal development objectives.

In RECBT, rigid and extreme attitudes are: (1) false, (2) illogical, and (3) unconstructive. In addition to rigid attitudes, there are three extreme attitudes that you need to understand; these are awfulising attitudes, discomfort intolerance attitudes and devaluation attitudes.

Rigid attitudes

When your coachee experiences an adversity – which is usually a negative event of some kind that serves as a potential obstacle to that person pursuing her personal development objective – she will healthily have a preference that this adversity did not happen. However, when she holds a rigid attitude towards the existence of the adversity, she transforms this preference into a rigid attitude (e.g. 'I would prefer that this adversity did not happen and therefore it absolutely should not have done so').

When Linda did not get her promised promotion, her rigid attitude was: 'My boss absolutely should have kept his promise to promote me.'

While rigid attitudes are based on a person's preferences, they are often expressed without the preference being made explicit. Thus instead of Linda saying: 'I want my boss to have kept his promise to promote me and therefore he absolutely should have done so', she says: 'My boss absolutely should have kept his promise to promote me.'

Your coachees can hold rigid attitudes towards themselves, other people and/or life conditions and these attitudes can be expressed using the following words: 'must', 'demand', 'absolutely should', 'have to', 'got to', to name but a few.

Extreme attitudes

In RECBT theory, rigid attitudes are at the very heart of your coachees' emotional problems and three extreme attitudes are derived from them which I will now discuss.
These are:

- awfulising attitudes
- discomfort intolerance attitudes, and
- devaluation attitudes.

Like rigid attitudes, these three extreme attitudes are deemed to be problematic because they are: (1) false, (2) illogical, and (3) unconstructive.

I will discuss these extreme attitudes one at a time.

Awfulising attitudes. When your coachee holds a rigid attitude towards an adversity, she will tend to hold an extreme awfulising attitude towards this adversity as well. This attitude is extreme in the sense that your coachee believes, at the time, one or more of the following:

- Nothing could be worse.
- The event in question is worse than 100% bad.
- No good could possibly come from this bad event.
- This event cannot be transcended or surmounted.

When your coachee experiences an adversity, she will healthily evaluate the relevant aspect of this adversity negatively. However, when she holds an extreme awfulising attitude towards the existence of the adversity, she transforms this negative evaluation into an awfulising attitude (e.g. 'It is bad that this adversity did happen and therefore it is awful that it did').

When Linda did not get her promised promotion, her extreme awfulising attitude was: 'It is awful that my boss absolutely did not keep his promise to promote me.'

While extreme awfulising attitudes are based on a person's negative evaluations, they are often expressed without the negative evaluations being made explicit. Thus instead of Linda saying: 'It is bad that my boss did not keep his promise to promote me and therefore it is awful that he did not do so', she says: 'It is awful that my boss did not keep his promise to promote me.'

Your coachees express extreme awfulising attitudes using the following words: 'it is terrible that…', 'it is awful that…', 'it is the end of the world that…', to name but a few.

Discomfort intolerance attitudes. When your coachee holds a rigid attitude towards an adversity, she will tend to hold an extreme discomfort intolerance attitude towards this adversity as well. This attitude is extreme in the sense that your coachee believes, at the time, one or more of the following:

- I will die or disintegrate if the adversity continues to exist. I can't tolerate it.

• I will lose the capacity to experience happiness if the adversity continues to exist.

When your coachee experiences an adversity, she will healthily consider it to be a struggle to tolerate this adversity. However, when she holds an extreme discomfort intolerance attitude towards the existence of the adversity, she transforms this sense of struggle into a discomfort intolerance attitude (e.g. 'It is a struggle for me to put up with the adversity and therefore I can't tolerate it').

When Linda did not get her promised promotion, her extreme discomfort intolerance attitude was: 'I can't tolerate the fact that my boss did not keep his promise to promote me.'

While extreme discomfort intolerance attitudes are based on a person's sense of struggle, they are often expressed without this sense being made explicit. Thus, instead of Linda saying: 'It is a struggle for me to put up with my boss not keeping his promise to promote me and therefore I can't tolerate it', she says: 'I can't tolerate the fact that my boss did not keep his promise to promote me.'

Your coachees express extreme discomfort tolerance attitudes using the following words: 'I can't stand it…', 'I can't tolerate it…', 'it is unbearable…', to name but a few.

Devaluation attitudes. When your coachee holds a rigid attitude towards an adversity, she will tend to hold an extreme devaluation attitude in relation to this adversity. The target of the devaluation attitude depends on who or what your coachee holds responsible for the adversity. Thus, if the coachee holds herself responsible for the adversity, she will hold a self-devaluation attitude; if she holds another or others responsible for the adversity, she will hold an other-devaluation attitude, and if she holds life responsible for the adversity, she will hold a life-devaluation attitude.

A devaluation attitude is extreme in the sense that your coachee believes, *at the time*, one or more of the following:

- A person (self or other) can legitimately be given a single global rating that defines their essence, and the worth of a person is dependent upon conditions that change (e.g. my worth goes up when I do well and goes down when I don't do well).
- The world can legitimately be given a single rating that defines its essential nature, and the value of the world varies according to what happens within it (e.g. the value of the world goes up when something fair occurs and goes down when something unfair happens).
- A person can be rated on the basis of one of his or her aspects and the world can be rated on the basis of one of its aspects.

When your coachee experiences an adversity, she will focus on this and healthily evaluate the relevant aspect negatively. However, when she holds an extreme devaluation attitude towards the existence of the adversity, she transforms this negative-aspect evaluation into a global negative evaluation of self, other or life depending on who or what your coachee holds responsible for the adversity (e.g. 'It is bad I brought about the adversity and therefore I am a bad person for doing so').

When Linda did not get her promised promotion, her extreme other-devaluation attitude was: 'My boss is a bad person for failing to keep his promise to promote me.'

While extreme devaluation attitudes are based on a person's negative evaluations of the adversity, they are often expressed without the negative evaluations being made explicit. Thus instead of Linda saying: 'It is bad that my boss did not keep his promise to promote me and therefore he is a bad person for not doing so', she says: 'My boss is a bad person for failing to keep his promise to promote me.'

It is important to note that when your coachees hold devaluation attitudes, they are assigning a global negative evaluation to self, to others or to life and these ratings are likely to vary according to the presence or absence of the adversities in question. Thus, Linda may evaluate her boss as a bad person for failing to keep his promise to promote her and as a good person if he kept his promise. It is also important to note that global evaluations occur on a continuum. Thus, Linda may not evaluate her boss as a bad person for failing to keep his promise but as less worthy for doing so. The latter is still an other-devaluation attitude even though Linda does not use the end-point of the global evaluation continuum since she still assigns her boss a global negative evaluation.

Understanding flexible and non-extreme attitudes

In explaining the role that flexible and non-extreme attitudes play in your coachees' healthy responses to obstacles to the pursuit of their personal development objectives, I will again illustrate my points by discussing the case of Linda who sought coaching because she was not being challenged in life. Remember that I helped her to set a number of personal development objectives that she prioritised and then began to work towards. Soon after, she failed to get promotion at work that had been promised to her by her boss. This adversity constituted a potential obstacle to her working towards her personal development objectives. In the previous section, I explained how Linda converted this potential obstacle into an actual one largely because of the rigid and extreme attitudes that she held about the obstacle. In this section, I will assume that Linda responded constructively to the potential obstacle, which enabled her to resume the pursuit of her personal development objectives. In doing so, I will highlight the flexible and non-extreme attitudes that were the foundation of this healthy response.

In RECBT, flexible and non-extreme attitudes are healthy because they are: (1) true, (2) logical, and (3) constructive. There are four such attitudes that you need to understand; these are flexible attitudes, non-awfulising attitudes, discomfort tolerance attitudes and unconditional acceptance attitudes.

Flexible attitudes

When your coachee experiences an adversity – which, as I said earlier, is usually a negative event of some kind that serves as a potential obstacle to that person pursuing her personal development objective – she will healthily have a preference that this adversity did not happen. However, in order for the person not to transform that preference into a rigid attitude towards the adversity and thus to keep the attitude flexible, she needs to negate any implicit demand that she might be making (e.g. 'I would prefer that this adversity did not happen, but that does not mean that it must not happen').

When Linda did not get her promised promotion, her flexible attitude was: 'I would have much preferred my boss to have kept his promise to promote me, but, sadly, he does not have to do what I want.' When a person expresses her preferences without explicitly negating her demand (e.g. 'I would have much preferred my boss to have kept his promise to promote me'), it is easy to conclude that the person is holding a flexible attitude. However, the only way to know for certain that the person's attitude is flexible or rigid is to consider whether or not the demand is explicitly negated. Thus, Linda could begin with her preference (i.e. 'I would have much preferred my boss to have kept his promise to promote me...') and easily transform this into a rigid attitude (i.e. '...and therefore he absolutely should have done so').

Thus, the only way to say with certainty that a person's attitude is flexible is when the person begins with their preference (e.g. 'I would have much preferred my boss to have kept his promise to promote me...') and then explicitly negates any implicit demand (e.g. '...but, sadly, he does not have to do what I want').

Your coachees can hold flexible attitudes towards themselves, other people and/or life conditions and these attitudes can be expressed using the following words: 'want', 'prefer', 'preferably should', 'it would be better', to name but a few. However, as discussed above, for these attitudes to be properly regarded as flexible, implicit demands need to be explicitly negated (e.g. 'but it does not have to be the way I want it to be', 'but there is no reason why it has to be', 'but it is not absolutely necessary').

In RECBT theory, flexible attitudes are at the very heart of your coachees' constructive responses to adversity and three attitudes, termed non-extreme attitudes, are derived from them. I will now discuss these.

They are:

- non-awfulising attitudes
- discomfort tolerance attitudes, and
- unconditional acceptance attitudes.

Like flexible attitudes, these three non-extreme attitudes are deemed to be healthy because they are: (1) true, (2) logical and (3) constructive.

I will discuss these non-extreme attitudes one at a time.

Non-awfulising attitudes. When your coachee holds a flexible attitude towards an adversity, she will tend to hold a non-extreme, non-awfulising attitude towards this adversity as well. This attitude is non-extreme in the sense that your coachee believes, at the time, one or more of the following:

- Things could always be worse.
- The event in question is less than 100% bad.
- Good could come from this bad event.
- This event can be transcended or surmounted.

When your coachee experiences an adversity, she will healthily evaluate the relevant aspect of this adversity negatively. However, in order for the person not to transform this negative evaluation into an extreme awfulising attitude towards the adversity and thus to keep the attitude non-extreme, she needs to negate any sense of awfulising (e.g. 'It is bad that this adversity happened, but not awful').

When Linda did not get her promised promotion her non-extreme, non-awfulising attitude was: 'It is bad that my boss did not keep his promise to promote me, but not awful.'

When a person expresses her non-awfulising attitude without explicitly negating the awfulising component (e.g. 'It is bad that my boss did not keep his promise to promote me'), it is easy to conclude that the person is holding a non-awfulising attitude. However, the only way to know for certain that the person's attitude is a non-extreme, non-awfulising one is to consider whether or not the awfulising component is negated. Thus, Linda could begin with her negative evaluation (i.e. 'It is bad that my boss did not keep his promise to promote me…') and easily transform this into an extreme awfulising attitude (i.e. '…and therefore it is awful').

Thus, the only way to say with certainty that a person's attitude is a non-extreme, non-awfulising one is when the person begins with their negative evaluation of the relevant aspect of this adversity (e.g. 'It is bad that my boss did not keep his promise to promote me…') and then explicitly negates any implicit awfulising component (e.g. '…but it isn't awful').

Your coachees can hold non-extreme, non-awfulising attitudes with reference to themselves, other people and/or life conditions and these attitudes can be expressed using the following words: 'it is bad that…', 'it is unfortunate that…', to name but two. However, as discussed above, for these attitudes to be properly regarded as non-extreme, the implicit awfulising components need to be explicitly negated (e.g. '...but it is not awful', 'but it is not the end of the world').

Discomfort tolerance attitudes. When your coachee holds a flexible attitude towards an adversity, she will tend to hold a non-extreme discomfort tolerance attitude towards her ability to withstand this adversity as well. This attitude is non-extreme in the sense that your coachee believes, at the time, one or more of the following:

- I will struggle if the discomfort continues to exist, but I will neither die nor disintegrate. I can tolerate such discomfort.
- I will not lose the capacity to experience happiness if the discomfort continues to exist, although this capacity will be temporarily diminished.
- The discomfort is worth tolerating.
- I am willing to tolerate it.
- I am going to tolerate it.

When your coachee experiences an adversity, she will healthily think that it is a struggle for her to withstand this adversity. However, in order for the person not to transform this healthy sense of struggle into an extreme discomfort intolerance attitude in relation to the adversity and thus to keep the attitude non-extreme, she needs to negate any sense of being unable to tolerate the discomfort of facing the adversity, indicate that it is in her interests to withstand the adversity (e.g. 'It is difficult for me to tolerate this adversity, but I can tolerate it and it is worth it to me to do so'), indicate that she is willing to tolerate the discomfort and state that she is going to tolerate it.

When Linda did not get her promised promotion, her non-extreme discomfort tolerance attitude was: 'It is a struggle for me to tolerate the fact that my boss did not keep his promise to promote me, but I can tolerate this, it is worth it to me to do so, I am willing to do so and I am going to do so.'

When a person expresses her discomfort tolerance attitude without explicitly negating the intolerance component (e.g. 'It is a struggle for me to tolerate the fact that my boss did not keep his promise to promote me'), it is easy to conclude that the person is holding a discomfort tolerance attitude. However, the only way to know for certain that the person's attitude is a non-extreme discomfort tolerance one is to consider whether or not (1) the intolerance component is negated, and (2) the 'worth it', willingness and action components are asserted. Thus, Linda could begin with her sense of struggle (i.e. 'It is a struggle for me to tolerate the fact that my boss did not keep his promise to promote me...') and easily transform this into an extreme discomfort intolerance attitude (i.e. '...and therefore I can't tolerate it').

Thus, the only way to say with certainty that a person's attitude is a non-extreme discomfort tolerance one is when the person:

- begins with their sense of struggle (e.g. 'It is a struggle for me to tolerate the fact that my boss did not keep his promise to promote me...')
- explicitly negates any implicit intolerance component (e.g. '... but I can tolerate this...')
- asserts the 'worth it' component (e.g. '...it is worth it to me to do so')
- asserts the 'willingness' component (e.g. '...I am willing to do so)
- asserts the 'action' component (e.g. '...and I am going to do so).

Your coachees can hold non-extreme discomfort tolerance attitudes with reference to themselves, other people and/or life conditions and these attitudes can be expressed using the following words: 'I can tolerate this', 'I can bear it', 'I can stand it', to name but a few. However, as discussed above, for these attitudes to be properly regarded as discomfort tolerance attitudes, the 'worth it', 'willingness' and 'action' components need to be made explicit (e.g. 'it is worth it to me to do so, I am willing to do so and I am going to do so'). Otherwise, the person may recognise theoretically that she can tolerate discomfort, but choose not to do so because (1) she cannot see that it is in her best interests to do so, (2) she is not willing to do so and/or (3) she is not going to do so.

Unconditional acceptance attitudes. When your coachee holds a flexible attitude towards an adversity, she will tend to hold a non-extreme, unconditional acceptance attitude in relation to this adversity. The target of the unconditional acceptance attitude depends on who or what your coachee holds responsible for the adversity. Thus, if the coachee holds herself responsible for the adversity, she will hold an unconditional self-acceptance attitude, if she holds another or others responsible for the adversity, she will hold an unconditional other-acceptance attitude and if she holds life responsible for the adversity, she will hold an unconditional life-acceptance attitude.

An unconditional acceptance attitude is non-extreme in the sense that your coachee believes, *at the time*, one or more of the following:

- A person cannot legitimately be given a single global rating that defines their essence, and their worth, as far as they have it, is not dependent upon conditions that change (e.g. my worth stays the same whether or not I do well).
- The world cannot legitimately be given a single rating that defines its essential nature, and the value of the world does not vary according to what happens within it (e.g. the value of the world stays the same whether fairness exists at any given time or not).
- It makes sense to rate discrete aspects of a person and of the world, but it does not make sense to rate a person or the world on the basis of these discrete aspects.

When your coachee experiences an adversity, she will focus on this and healthily evaluate the relevant aspect of this adversity negatively. As mentioned above, this aspect may be to do with oneself, another person or persons or life conditions. However, in order for the person not to transform this negative evaluation into an extreme devaluation attitude towards the adversity and thus to keep the attitude non-extreme, she needs to negate any sense of devaluation (e.g. 'It is bad that I brought about this adversity, but I am fallible for doing so and not a bad person').

When Linda did not get her promised promotion, her non-extreme, unconditional other-acceptance attitude was: 'It is bad that my boss failed to keep his promise to promote me, but he is not a bad person for failing to do so. Rather, he is a fallible, unrateable human being who did the wrong thing.'

When a person expresses her acceptance attitude while negating the devaluation component (e.g. 'It is bad that my boss failed to keep his promise to promote me, but he is not a bad person for failing to do so...'), it is easy to conclude that the person is holding an acceptance attitude (in this case an other-acceptance attitude). However, the only way to know for certain that the person's attitude is a non-extreme, acceptance one is to consider whether or not (1) the devaluation component is negated, and (2) the acceptance component is asserted. Thus, Linda could begin with negating the other-devaluation component (i.e. 'It is bad that my boss failed to keep his promise to promote me, but he is not a bad person for failing to do so...') and easily transform this into an extreme devaluation component whereby the worth of the person still varies (e.g. '...however, he would be worthier if he kept his promise than if he broke it').

Thus, the only way to say with certainty that a person's attitude is a non-extreme acceptance one is when the person:

- begins with negatively evaluating the relevant aspect (e.g. 'It is bad that my boss failed to keep his promise to promote me...')

- explicitly negates any implicit devaluation component (e.g. '...but he is not a bad person for failing to do so...') and
- asserts the 'acceptance' component (e.g. '...rather, he is a fallible, unrateable human being who did the wrong thing').

This is why Albert Ellis (2005) referred to such attitudes as *unconditional* acceptance attitudes because, in this case for example, Linda's boss is accepted unconditionally as a fallible, unrateable person whose worth (if he can be said to have it) does not change in the light of his changing behaviour.

Your coachees can hold non-extreme, unconditional acceptance attitudes with reference to themselves, other people and/or life conditions. When unconditional acceptance attitudes refer to a person (self or others), the following words (or synonyms) should be used: 'I am (or you are) fallible, unrateable, complex and in flux.' If the concept of worth is to be used, then it should be made clear that such 'worth' is a given about the person and does not change in his or her lifetime. Thus the unconditional aspect of self-acceptance and other-acceptance should preferably be emphasised here.

When unconditional acceptance attitudes refer to life, the following words (or synonyms) should be used: 'Life is a complex mixture of good, bad and neutral aspects, too complex to be given a single rating.' Again, if the concept of worth is to be used with respect to life, then it should be made clear once more that such 'worth' is a given about life and does not change according to changing circumstances. The unconditional aspect of life-acceptance should again preferably be emphasised here.

Note

1   Ellis referred to these attitudes as 'beliefs', but I think that the term 'attitudes' is a more accurate one in explaining the evaluative nature of the cognitions that are at the foundation of psychological disturbance and health. I will use the term 'attitudes' throughout this book rather than 'beliefs' (see Dryden, 2016, for a full discussion of this issue).

Part 2

Understanding your coachees' common emotional problems and their healthy alternatives

The 'situational ABC' framework

In the previous part of this book, I discussed rigid and extreme attitudes and their flexible and non-extreme alternatives. I made the point that rigid and extreme attitudes are at the core of your coachees' disturbed responses to life's adversities and that flexible and non-extreme attitudes are at the core of their constructive responses to the same negative events. RECBT outlines a 'situational ABC' framework that I will use in helping you to understand your coachees' emotional problems and their healthy alternatives. In this framework, 'A' stands for the Adversity that your coachee is facing or thinks she is facing, 'B' stands for the Basic Attitudes[1] that your coachee holds towards this actual or perceived adversity and 'C' stands for the Consequences of holding these attitudes. These consequences are emotional, behavioural and cognitive in nature. In this part of the book, I will consider both problematic and constructive emotional responses to adversities before showing how you can help your coachees deal effectively with the former and experience the latter in Parts 3 and 4 of the book.

It is a fundamental view of RECBT theory that when your coachee experiences an adversity, it is constructive for her to experience a healthy negative emotion (which I refer to as an HNE) since doing so enables her to process the experience emotionally, make sense of what has happened to her and move on with her life. You only need to help your coachee deal with a life adversity in coaching when she experiences an unhealthy negative emotion (known as a UNE) in response to this adversity and gets stuck as a result. This latter point is very important. If your coachee first experiences a problematic or unhealthy emotion about an adversity, but then regroups and deals with it effectively later, you do not need to intervene since your coachee has got herself back on the path of working towards her personal development objectives. However, if she has responded to an adversity with a problematic negative emotion, remains stuck in this mode and cannot bypass it, then she requires your intervention. However, to reiterate a point that I made earlier, you should only do this if you are trained and sufficiently skilled to do so.

'A' stands for adversity

Earlier I mentioned the work of Albert Ellis, the founder of rational emotive behaviour therapy, who distinguished carefully between rigid and extreme attitudes and flexible and non-extreme attitudes. When understanding what constitutes an adversity for your coachee, we need to draw on the work of another giant in the field of cognitive behaviour therapy (CBT), Aaron T. Beck, who introduced the concept of the personal domain (Beck, 1976).

Beck thought of the personal domain as a kind of psychological space that contains anything that the person deems to be personally valuable. An adversity can thus be seen as a negative event that has a particular relation to the person's personal domain as perceived by the person herself. In my view there are two major parts of the personal domain: that which relates to the person's sense of worth or ego (the ego part of the domain) and that which relates to those things that the person values which do not relate to the person's sense of worth or ego (the non-ego part of the domain). Thus, as we shall presently see, a person may feel anxiety or concerned when she perceives a threat to either the ego or non-ego part of her personal domain.

As this example shows, an adversity on its own at 'A' does not tell us whether the person's emotional response to it is unhealthy or healthy (we need to know whether the person holds rigid and extreme or flexible and non-extreme attitudes to know that). However, when we know the theme of an adversity (e.g. threat), we at least know that the person will either experience an unhealthy negative emotion (e.g. anxiety in the case of threat) or a healthy negative emotion (e.g. concern in the case of threat). Later in this part of the book, I will discuss eight pairs of emotions and show how they relate to different adversity themes.

'C' stands for consequences

'C' in the 'ABC' framework stands for the consequences that the person experiences when she holds a basic attitude (at 'B') about the adversity (at 'A'). There are three major sets of consequences that we need to consider: emotional consequences, behavioural consequences and thinking consequences. We already know that the emotional consequence of rigid and extreme attitudes towards an adversity is likely to be negative and problematic (i.e. a UNE). Whereas when the person holds a set of flexible and non-extreme attitudes towards the same adversity, then her emotion is likely to be negative and constructive (i.e. an HNE).

In similar vein, when the person holds a set of rigid and extreme attitudes towards the adversity, her behavioural consequences will be unconstructive (i.e. she is likely to behave in an unconstructive way) and her thinking consequences will be unconstructive (i.e. she will subsequently think in a highly distorted and negative manner). When she experiences such unconstructive behavioural and thinking consequences, these combined with the associated unhealthy emotional consequences will lead the person to become stuck. She will require your help to refocus on her coaching objectives if she is stuck and if she cannot bypass her emotional problem sufficiently to pursue these objectives.

However, when the person holds a set of flexible and non-extreme attitudes towards the adversity, her behavioural consequences will be constructive (i.e. she is likely to behave in a constructive way) and her thinking consequences will be constructive (i.e. she will subsequently think in a realistic and balanced manner). Together with her healthy emotional response her subsequent behaviour and thinking will enable her to process the adversity effectively and move on.

I will bring all these 'ABC' components together in detailing the eight common emotional problems that you will encounter in coaching and their healthy alternatives. In doing so, I will discuss the factors involved in both the emotional problem and its healthy alternative and will provide you with a tabular summary of the differences between unhealthy negative emotions (UNEs) and healthy negative emotions (HNEs).

Before I begin, I want to make an important observation on emotions and the labels we give to them.

Emotions and the labels we give to them

A central plank of RECBT theory of emotional problems and their solutions is that when your coachee faces an adversity – either one that can be objectively verified or one that she interprets personally as an adversity – then she is bound to experience a negative emotion. When she is bogged down with this emotional response accompanied by associated behavioural and thinking responses, then this emotion is likely to be negative in tone and unhealthy in consequence. We call these emotions unhealthy negative emotions (or UNEs) in RECBT theory.

Alternatively, when your coachee experiences a negative emotion about this adversity but is not bogged down by it and can get on with her life, albeit with some difficulty, then this negative emotion will be accompanied by a different set of behavioural and thinking responses that aid recovery. We call these emotions healthy negative emotions (or HNEs) in RECBT theory.

It is important for you to note when I discuss these emotions that we do not, as humans, have a universally agreed and accepted lexicon when it comes to emotions. What appear below are comparisons between pairs of UNEs and HNEs. Please remember throughout what follows that the labels I have given the eight pairs of emotions are my own and should not be uncritically used in coaching practice.

What is important when you are working with a coachee on the emotional problem that she is stuck with, and which serves as an obstacle to her progress towards her personal development objectives, is that you develop a shared understanding of which label you are going to give to her major UNE and to her HNE alternative. You may, of course, use the language that I employ below as a starting off point, but it is good coaching practice to end up with agreed emotional terms that you can both use to differentiate your coachee's UNE from the HNE, which hopefully comprises her emotional goal that you are going to help her achieve. I discuss this issue from a more practical perspective in Steps 4 and 9 in the guide that appears in Part 3 of this book. With this caveat, let me discuss the eight unhealthy negative emotions (Dryden, 2009), one of which is very likely to feature in your coachee's emotional problems, and their eight healthy alternatives. In doing so, I will not cover all possible features of these emotions, just their main features.

Anxiety and concern

As I mentioned above, when your coachee has an emotional problem where anxiety predominates, then the adversity that features at 'A' in the 'ABC' framework will be some kind of threat to her personal domain. This threat may be deemed to be to her self-esteem or broadly speaking to the non-ego domain of her sense of comfort. Albert Ellis (1979, 1980) used the terms 'ego anxiety and discomfort anxiety' to distinguish between these two forms of anxiety.

From an RECBT theoretical perspective, it is important to bear in mind that threat-based adversity does not, on its own, bring about your coachee's anxiety. Rather, it is the rigid and extreme attitudes that she holds towards this adversity that are at the core of her anxiety response. Aside from the emotional part of this response, when your coachee is anxious her behaviour will be dominated by a wish to escape from this threat as quickly as possible or seek safety if she cannot escape physically from it. In addition, her subsequent thinking will exaggerate the nature of the threat and its consequences/implications and because these thoughts (in words or in images) will be vivid, and backed up by increased anxious feeling, your coachee may well think that they have a predictive quality. In other words, your coachee will operate on the principle at this point that 'if I think it, then it is likely to happen'. As is outlined in Table 1, when your coachee experiences anxiety, her thinking may also be characterised by safety-seeking thinking. Frequently, coachees alternate between threat-exaggerated thinking and safety-seeking thinking when they are anxious.

Your coaching goal is to help your coachee deal with this threat in a healthier manner so that she can get 'unstuck' and move on with her life, including resuming the work that she had started with you pursuing her personal development objectives.

In RECBT theory, we regard concern (or whatever emotional term you and your coachee have agreed to use) as the healthy alternative to anxiety in dealing with a threat-based adversity. Concern, from an RECBT theoretical perspective, stems from a set of flexible and non-extreme attitudes towards threat-based adversity. Aside from the emotional part of this response, when your coachee is concerned, but not anxious, she will be inclined, behaviourally, to face up to and deal with the threat rather than

Table 1 Anxiety vs. concern

Adversity	• You are facing a threat to your personal domain	
Basic attitude	**RIGID AND EXTREME**	**FLEXIBLE AND NON-EXTREME**
Emotion	**Anxiety**	**Concern**
Behaviour	• You avoid the threat • You withdraw physically from the threat • You ward off the threat (e.g. by rituals or superstitious behaviour) • You try to neutralise the threat (e.g. by being nice to people of whom you are afraid) • You distract yourself from the threat by engaging in other activity • You keep checking on the current status of the threat hoping to find that it has disappeared or become benign • You seek reassurance from others that the threat is benign • You seek support from others so that if the threat happens, they will handle it or be there to rescue you • You overprepare in order to minimise the threat happening or so that you are prepared to meet it (NB it is the overpreparation that is the problem here)	• You face up to the threat without using any safety-seeking measures • You take constructive action to deal with the threat • You seek support from others to help you face up to the threat and then take constructive actiwon by yourself rather than rely on them to handle it for you or to be there to rescue you • You prepare to meet the threat but do not overprepare

(continued)

Table 1 Cont.

	• You tranquillise your feelings so that you don't think about the threat • You overcompensate for feeling vulnerable by seeking out an even greater threat to prove to yourself that you can cope	
Subsequent thinking	*Threat-exaggerated thinking* • You overestimate the probability of the threat occurring • You underestimate your ability to cope with the threat • You ruminate about the threat • You create an even more negative threat in your mind • You magnify the negative consequences of the threat and minimise its positive consequences • You have more task-irrelevant thoughts than in concern *Safety-seeking thinking* • You withdraw mentally from the threat • You try to persuade yourself that the threat is not imminent and that you are 'imagining' it • You think in ways designed to reassure yourself that the threat is benign or, if not, that its consequences will be insignificant	• You are realistic about the probability of the threat occurring • You view the threat realistically • You realistically appraise your ability to cope with the threat • You think about what to do concerning dealing with the threat constructively rather than ruminate about the threat • You have more task-relevant thoughts than in anxiety • You picture yourself dealing with the threat in a realistic way

Table I Cont.

	• You distract yourself from the threat, e.g. by focusing on mental scenes of safety and well-being	
	• You overprepare mentally in order to minimise the threat happening or so that you are prepared to meet it (NB once again it is the overpreparation that is the problem here)	
	• You picture yourself dealing with the threat in a masterful way	
	• You overcompensate for your feeling of vulnerability by picturing yourself dealing effectively with an even bigger threat	

escape from it. Her subsequent thinking will be realistic and balanced in nature rather than highly distorted and skewed as in anxiety.

If you can help your coachee to develop a flexible and non-extreme attitude towards the threat, and encourage her to act and think in ways that are consistent with her flexible and non-extreme attitude, then you will not only help her to be healthily concerned rather than anxious about her threat-based adversity, but also help her to get unstuck and move on with her life, including resuming her coaching work towards her personal development objectives. Table 1 reviews, in full, the major features of anxiety and concern. You will see from the table that the 'A' is the same for both emotions, but the 'B' and 'C' are different. This is true for all eight pairs of emotions that I will discuss in this part of the book.

Depression[2] and sadness

When your coachee has an emotional problem where depression predominates, then the adversity that features at 'A' in the 'ABC' framework will be some kind of loss or failure within your coachee's personal domain or some kind of undeserved plight suffered by self or others. This loss, failure or undeserved plight may again be deemed to be to her self-esteem or broadly speaking to the non-ego domain of her sense of comfort.

Again from an RECBT theoretical perspective, it is important to bear in mind that loss-based, failure-based or undeserved plight-based adversity does not, on its own, bring about your coachee's depression. Rather, it is the rigid and extreme attitudes that she holds about this adversity that are at the core of her depressive response. Aside from the emotional part of this response, when your coachee is depressed her behaviour will be dominated by a wish to withdraw into herself and away from what was previously experienced as enjoyable. There is a general shutting down of ordinary responsiveness. In addition, her subsequent thinking will be characterised by memories of past losses or failures and a general sense of helplessness and, in extreme cases, of depression and hopelessness.

Aaron T. Beck, who coined the term 'personal domain' (Beck, 1976), has made a useful distinction between autonomy-related depression and sociotropy-related depression. If your coachee experiences autonomy-related depression, she is depressed about a loss, failure or undeserved plight within that part of her domain in which her sense of autonomy, effectiveness, competence is highly prized. Examples of autonomy-related self-attitudes related to depression are: 'I am weak', 'I am defective' and 'I am a failure', and the conditions and the non-ego conditions that your coachee believes she cannot tolerate include being dependent on others, having one's sense of freedom restrained and being unable to achieve one's valued goals.

On the other hand, if your coachee experiences sociotropy-related depression, she is depressed about a loss, failure or undeserved plight within that part of her domain in which her connection to others and how others see her are highly prized. Examples of sociotropy-related self-attitudes related to depression are: 'I am unlovable', 'I am unlikeable' and 'I am worthless', and the non-ego conditions that your coachee believes she cannot tolerate include not having someone on whom one can depend, being alone and being rejected.

Your coaching goal is again to help your coachee deal with loss, failure or undeserved plight in a healthier manner so that she can get unstuck and move on with her life, including resuming the work that she had started with you pursuing her personal development objectives.

Sadness is deemed to be the healthy alternative to depression (although the important point here is the term you and your coachee have agreed to use as the healthy alternative to depression) and, from an RECBT theoretical perspective, it stems from a set of flexible and non-extreme attitudes towards loss-based, failure-based or undeserved plight-based adversity. Aside from the emotional part of this response, when your coachee is sad, but not depressed, she will be inclined, behaviourally, to stay connected to the world rather than withdraw from it. Her subsequent thinking will be realistic and balanced in nature rather than highly distorted and skewed as in depression.

If you can help your coachee to develop flexible and non-extreme attitudes towards loss, failure or undeserved plight, and can encourage her to act and think in ways that are consistent with these attitudes, then you will not only help her to be healthily sad rather than depressed about her loss-based, failure-based or undeserved plight-based adversity, but also help her to get unstuck and move on with her life, including resuming her coaching work towards her personal development objectives. Table 2 reviews, in full, the major features of depression and sadness.

Table 2 Depression vs. sadness

Adversity	• You have experienced a loss from the sociotropic and/or autonomous realms of your personal domain • You have experienced failure within the sociotropic and/or autonomous realms of your personal domain • You or others have experienced an undeserved plight	
Basic attitude	**RIGID AND EXTREME**	**FLEXIBLE AND NON-EXTREME**
Emotion	**Depression**	**Sadness**
Behaviour	• You become overly dependent on and seek to cling to others (particularly in sociotropic depression) • You bemoan your fate or that of others to anyone who will listen (particularly in pity-based depression) • You create an environment consistent with your depressed feelings • You attempt to terminate feelings of depression in self-destructive ways • You either push away attempts to comfort you (in autonomous depression) or use such comfort to reinforce your dependency (in sociotropic depression) or your self- or other-pity (in pity-based depression)	• You seek out reinforcements after a period of mourning (particularly when your inferential theme is loss) • You create an environment inconsistent with depressed feelings • You express your feelings about the loss, failure or undeserved plight and talk in a non-complaining way about these feelings to significant others • You allow yourself to be comforted in a way that helps you to express your feelings of sadness and mourn your loss
Subsequent thinking	• You see only negative aspects of the loss, failure or undeserved plight • You think of other losses, failures and undeserved plights that you (and, in the case of the latter, others) have experienced	• You are able to recognise both negative and positive aspects of the loss or failure • You think you are able to help yourself • You look to the future with hope

Table 2 Cont.

	• You think you are unable to help yourself (helplessness)	
	• You only see pain and blackness in the future (hopelessness)	
	• You see yourself as being totally dependent on others (in autonomous depression)	
	• You see yourself as being disconnected from others (in sociotropic depression)	
	• You see the world as full of undeservedness and unfairness (in plight-based depression)	
	• You tend to ruminate concerning the source of your depression and its consequences	

Guilt and remorse

When your coachee has an emotional problem where guilt predominates, then the adversity that features at 'A' in the 'ABC' framework will be a violation of her moral code, a failure to live up to her moral code or where the person has hurt the feelings of another person or persons. As with other emotions, a rigid attitude and an extreme attitude of, in the case of guilt, self-devaluation mediate between the above themes at 'A' and the emotion of guilt at 'C'. Indeed, guilt is one of only two UNEs that is based exclusively on self-devaluation (shame is the other). In guilt, the self-devaluation concerns one's badness.

Aside from the emotional part of this response, when your coachee feels guilt, her behaviour will be dominated by a wish to beg for forgiveness along with the sense that she does not deserve to be forgiven. In addition, her subsequent thinking will exaggerate the threat of retribution from others or by some deity.

Remorse is, from an RECBT theoretical perspective, deemed to be the healthy alternative to guilt (although again the important issue here is the term you and your coachee have agreed to use as the healthy alternative to guilt). It stems from a set of flexible and non-extreme attitudes towards doing the wrong thing, failing to do the right thing or hurting someone. Aside from the emotional part of this response, when your coachee feels remorse, rather than guilt, she will be inclined, behaviourally, to look for forgiveness rather than begging for it, accompanied by the sense that she is worthy of forgiveness. Her subsequent thinking will be realistic and balanced in nature and relate to one being penalised rather than receiving divine or human retribution as in guilt.

As with other emotions, your task is to help your coachee to develop a flexible and non-extreme attitude towards moral code violations and to encourage her to act and think in ways that are consistent with her flexible and non-extreme attitude. If she feels remorse rather than guilt, she will be able to come to terms with what she did (or failed to do) and resume her coaching work towards her personal development objectives. Table 3 reviews, in full, the major features of guilt and remorse.

Shame and disappointment

When your coachee has an emotional problem where shame predominates, then the adversity that features at 'A' in the 'ABC' framework will be a drastic falling short of a valued standard perpetrated by herself or by a member of a social group with which your coachee closely identifies, together with a sense (which may or may not reflect reality) that your coachee and/or the group involved is being devalued by relevant judging observers. As with other emotions, a rigid attitude and an extreme attitude of, in the case of shame, self-devaluation mediate between the above themes at 'A' and the emotion of shame. In shame, the self-devaluation concerns one's defectiveness, disgracefulness or a sense of being diminished either as a result of your coachee's own

Table 3 Guilt vs. remorse

Adversity	• You have broken your moral code • You have failed to live up to your moral code • You have hurt someone's feelings	
Basic attitude	**RIGID AND EXTREME**	**FLEXIBLE AND NON-EXTREME**
Emotion	**Guilt**	**Remorse**
Behaviour	• You escape from the unhealthy pain of guilt in self-defeating ways • You beg forgiveness from the person you have wronged • You promise unrealistically that you will not 'sin' again • You punish yourself physically or by deprivation • You defensively disclaim responsibility for wrongdoing • You make excuses for your behaviour • You reject offers of forgiveness	• You face up to the healthy pain that accompanies the realisation that you have sinned • You ask, but do not beg, for forgiveness • You understand the reasons for your wrongdoing and act on your understanding • You atone for the sin by taking a penalty • You make appropriate amends • You do not make excuses for your behaviour or enact other defensive behaviour • You accept offers for forgiveness
Subsequent thinking	• You conclude that you have definitely committed the sin • You assume more personal responsibility than the situation warrants • You assign far less responsibility to others than is warranted • You dismiss possible mitigating factors for your behaviour • You only see your behaviour in a guilt-related context and fail to put it into an overall context • You think that you will receive retribution	• You take into account all relevant data when judging whether or not you have 'sinned' • You assume an appropriate level of personal responsibility • You assign an appropriate level of responsibility to others • You take into account mitigating factors • You put your behaviour into overall context • You think you may be penalised rather than receive retribution

behaviour or through membership of the 'shamed' social group with whom she identifies.

Aside from the emotional part of this response, when your coachee feels shame, her behaviour will be dominated by a wish to disappear from the judgemental gaze of the observing group. In addition, her subsequent thinking will exaggerate the extent of social scorn and exclusion and the perceived implications of such social condemnation.

Disappointment is, from an RECBT theoretical perspective, deemed to be the healthy alternative to shame (although again the important point here is the term you and your coachee have agreed to use as the healthy alternative to shame). It stems from a set of flexible and non-extreme attitudes towards an observed and negatively judged significant falling short of a valued standard by self or closely identified other. Aside from the emotional part of this response, when your coachee feels disappointed, rather than ashamed, she will be inclined, behaviourally, to look at the judging group and engage in a dialogue about the possible reasons for her behaviour or that of the closely identified other, accompanied by the sense that she is not defective, disgraceful or diminished as a person. Her subsequent thinking will be realistic and balanced in nature and relate to the broad range of responses from the judging group and the time-limited nature of any social censure or exclusion.

As with other emotions, your task is to help your coachee to develop a flexible and non-extreme attitude towards drastic falls from 'grace' and to encourage her to act and think in ways that are consistent with her flexible and non-extreme attitude. If she feels disappointed rather than ashamed, she will be able to come to terms with her behaviour or that of the closely identified other and resume her coaching work towards her personal development objectives. Table 4 reviews, in full, the major features of shame and disappointment.

Table 4 Shame vs. disappointment

Adversity	• Something highly negative has been revealed about you (or about a group with whom you identify) by yourself or by others • You have acted in a way that falls very short of your ideal • Others look down on or shun you (or a group with whom you identify) or you think that they do	
Basic attitude	**RIGID AND EXTREME**	**FLEXIBLE AND NON-EXTREME**
Emotion	**Shame**	**Disappointment**
Behaviour	• You remove yourself from the 'gaze' of others • You isolate yourself from others • You save face by attacking other(s) who have 'shamed' you • You defend your threatened self-esteem in self-defeating ways • You ignore attempts by others to restore social equilibrium	• You continue to participate actively in social interaction • You respond positively to attempts of others to restore social equilibrium
Subsequent thinking	• You overestimate the negativity of the information revealed • You overestimate the likelihood that the judging group will notice or be interested in the information • You overestimate the degree of disapproval you (or your reference group) will receive • You overestimate how long any disapproval will last	• You see the information revealed in a compassionate self-accepting context • You are realistic about the likelihood that the judging group will notice or be interested in the information revealed • You are realistic about the degree of disapproval you (or your reference group) will receive • You are realistic about how long any disapproval will last

Hurt and sorrow

When your coachee has an emotional problem where feelings of hurt predominate, then the adversity that features at 'A' in the 'ABC' framework will be a sense of her being let down by a significant other where she considers herself undeserving of such treatment or where she is more invested in the relationship than is the other. As with other emotions, a rigid attitude and an extreme attitude mediate between the above theme at 'A' and the emotion of hurt. In hurt, your coachee either feels sorry for herself (non-ego hurt) or considers herself worth less as a result of such treatment (ego hurt).

Aside from the emotional part of this response, when your coachee feels hurt, her behaviour will be dominated by a wish to stop communicating directly with the person who she sees as having 'hurt' her. Having said this, your coachee may well also seek ways of communicating her feelings indirectly to the other, mainly by sulking. In addition, her subsequent thinking will exaggerate the extent of the bad treatment and she will think of ways to make the person suffer.

Sorrow is, from an RECBT theoretical perspective, deemed to be the healthy alternative to hurt (although, as before, the important point here is the term you and your coachee have agreed to use as the healthy alternative to hurt). It stems from a set of flexible and non-extreme attitudes towards undeserved bad treatment from a significant other and where the person feels more invested in the relationship than is the other. Aside from the emotional part of this response, when your coachee feels sorrowful, rather than hurt, she will be inclined, behaviourally, to communicate her feelings of sorrow directly to the other person. Her subsequent thinking will be realistic and balanced in nature and place the person's behaviour into a broader context where humans are not immune from treating one another badly, even those close to them, and where in life it does happen that people have different levels of investment in a relationship.

As with other emotions, your task is to help your coachee to develop a flexible and non-extreme attitude towards undeserved bad treatment from a significant other and to encourage her to act and think in ways that are consistent with her flexible and non-extreme attitude. If she feels sorrowful rather than hurt, she will be able to come to terms with the behaviour of the other person and resume her coaching work towards her personal development objectives. Table 5 reviews, in full, the major features of hurt and sorrow.

Problematic anger and constructive anger

When your coachee has an emotional problem where problematic anger predominates, then the adversity that features at 'A' in the 'ABC' framework will be a transgression of one of your coachee's important rules by self (problematic anger at self) or by another (problematic anger at another) or an attack on her self-esteem by someone. In this section, I will concentrate on anger at another person or persons. As with other emotions, a rigid attitude and an extreme attitude mediate between the above theme at 'A' and the emotion of problematic anger, although your coachee will often cling to the idea that the other (in particular) caused her problematic anger directly.

Aside from the emotional part of this response, when your coachee feels problematic anger, her behaviour will be dominated by a wish to attack the other either physically or psychologically along with a desire to suppress this tendency. When this suppression fails or is bypassed, problematic anger is transformed into aggression. In addition, your coachee's subsequent thinking will exaggerate the malicious intent of the other and she will be preoccupied with thoughts of revenge.

Constructive anger is, from an RECBT theoretical perspective, deemed to be the healthy alternative to problematic anger (although, as I have consistently said, the important point here is the term you and your coachee have agreed to use as the healthy

Table 5 Hurt vs. sorrow

Adversity	• Others treat you badly (and you think you do not deserve such treatment) • You think that the other person is less invested in your relationship than you are	
Basic attitude	**RIGID AND EXTREME**	**FLEXIBLE AND NON-EXTREME**
Emotion	**Hurt**	**Sorrow**
Behaviour	• You stop communicating with the other person • You sulk and make obvious you feel hurt without disclosing details of the matter • You indirectly criticise or punish the other person for their offence • You tell others how badly you have been treated, but don't take any responsibility for any contribution you may have made to this	• You communicate your feelings to the other directly • You request that the other person acts in a fairer manner towards you • You discuss the situation with others in a balanced manner, focusing on the way you have been treated and taking responsibility for any contribution you may have made to this
Subsequent thinking	• You overestimate the unfairness of the other person's behaviour • You think that the other person does not care for you or is indifferent to you • You see yourself as alone, uncared for or misunderstood • You tend to think of past 'hurts' • You think that the other person has to make the first move to you and you dismiss the possibility of making the first move towards that person	• You are realistic about the degree of unfairness in the other person's behaviour • You think that the other person has acted badly rather than demonstrated indifference or lack of caring • You see yourself as being in a poor situation, but still connected to, cared for by and understood by others not directly involved in the situation • If you think of past hurts, you do so with less frequency and less intensity than when you feel hurt • You are open to the idea of making the first move towards the other person

alternative to problematic anger). It stems from a set of flexible and non-extreme attitudes towards the other transgressing your coachee's important rule or attacking her self-esteem. Aside from the emotional part of this response, when your coachee feels constructive anger, rather than problematic anger, she will be inclined, behaviourally, to communicate her feelings of displeasure directly to the other person from the position of demonstrating acceptance of the other. This is nicely summed up by a quote attributed to Voltaire, who was reported to say to someone: 'Sir, I disapprove of what you say, but I will defend to the death your right to say it.' When constructively angry, your coachee's subsequent thinking will again be realistic and balanced in nature and she will think about how best to assert herself with the other person rather than punish him or her.

As with other emotions, your task is to help your coachee to develop a flexible and non-extreme attitude towards the other's rule transgressing and self-esteem attacking behaviour. In rule transgression the non-extreme attitude will most likely be an unconditional other-acceptance attitude, whereas when the other attacks your coachee's self-esteem she needs to hold both an unconditional other-acceptance attitude and an unconditional self-acceptance attitude. You also need to encourage her to act and think in ways that are consistent with her flexible and non-extreme attitudes. If she feels constructively angry rather than problematically angry, she will be able to come to terms with the behaviour of the other person and resume her coaching work towards her personal development objectives. Table 6 reviews, in full, the major features of problematic anger and constructive anger.

Problematic jealousy[3] and constructive jealousy

When your coachee has an emotional problem where problematic jealousy predominates, then the adversity that features at 'A' in the 'ABC' framework will be an inferred threat to an important relationship with a prized other. As with other emotions, a rigid

Table 6 Problematic anger vs. constructive anger

Adversity	• You think that you have been frustrated in some way or your movement towards an important goal has been obstructed in some way • Someone has treated you badly • Someone has transgressed one of your personal rules • You have transgressed one of your own personal rules • Someone or something has threatened your self-esteem or disrespected you	
Basic attitude	**RIGID AND EXTREME**	**FLEXIBLE AND NON-EXTREME**
Emotion	**Problematic anger**	**Constructive anger**
Behaviour	• You attack the other(s) physically • You attack the other(s) verbally • You attack the other(s) passive-aggressively • You displace the attack on to another person, animal or object • You withdraw aggressively • You recruit allies against the other(s)	• You assert yourself with the other(s) • You request, but do not demand, behavioural change from the other(s) • You leave an unsatisfactory situation non-aggressively after taking steps to deal with it
Subsequent thinking`	• You overestimate the extent to which the other(s) acted deliberately • You see malicious intent in the motives of the other(s) • You see yourself as definitely right and the other(s) as definitely wrong • You are unable to see the point of view of the other(s) • You plot to exact revenge • You ruminate about the other's behaviour and imagine coming out on top	• You think that the other(s) may have acted deliberately, but you also recognise that this may not have been the case • You are able to see the point of view of the other(s) • You have fleeting, rather than sustained, thoughts to exact revenge • You think that other(s) may have had malicious intent in their motives, but you also recognise that this may not have been the case • You think that you are probably rather than definitely right and the other(s) probably rather than definitely wrong

attitude and an extreme attitude mediate between the above theme at 'A' and the emotion of problematic jealousy. In problematic jealousy, your coachee finds uncertainty about what the person with whom she is involved is doing or thinking intolerable (non-ego features of problematic jealousy) and considers herself less worthy than potential rivals of the affections of the other with whom she is involved (ego features of problematic jealousy)

Aside from the emotional part of this response, when your coachee feels problematically jealous, her behaviour will be dominated by a wish to prevent the other from relating with potential rivals or to monitor the behaviour and thinking of the other person when he is in the company of women. In addition, her subsequent thinking will exaggerate the meaning of any contact between the person and her rivals and will elaborate though imagery the threat contained in such contact.

Constructive jealousy (sometimes referred to as 'concern for one's relationship') is, from an RECBT theoretical perspective, deemed to be the healthy alternative to problematic jealousy (once again, the important point here is the term you and your coachee have agreed to use as the healthy alternative to problematic jealousy). It stems from a set of flexible and non-extreme attitudes towards an inferred threat to your coachee's relationship with a prized other. Aside from the emotional part of this response, when your coachee feels constructive jealousy, rather than problematic jealousy, she will be inclined, behaviourally, to (1) tolerate uncertainty and not check on the activities of the other, for example, and where there is evidence of a threat to her relationship to (2) communicate her concerns directly to the other person. Her subsequent thinking will again be realistic and balanced in nature and will locate the person's behaviour within a non-threatening context. There will also be no mental elaborations of any threatening aspects of contact between the prized person and any rivals. Indeed, in constructive jealousy, others are not deemed to be rivals unless there is clear, objective evidence to think of them as such.

As with other emotions, your task is to help your coachee to develop a flexible and non-extreme attitude towards inferred threats to her relationship with a prized other and to encourage her to act and think in ways that are consistent with her flexible and non-extreme attitude. If she feels constructively jealous rather than problematically jealous, she will be able to be objective about the existence of a threat to her relationship and to go along with the probability that such a threat does not exist unless she has clear evidence of its existence, and to come to terms with the threat if it does exist. In both cases, your coachee will be able to resume her coaching work towards her personal development objectives. Table 7 reviews, in full, the major features of problematic jealousy and constructive jealousy.

Problematic envy and constructive envy

When your coachee has an emotional problem where problematic envy predominates, then the adversity that features at 'A' in the 'ABC' framework will be another person having something (e.g. an object or relationship) that your coachee prizes, does not have, but wants. For the last time, as with the other emotions that I have discussed, a rigid attitude and an extreme attitude mediate between the above theme at 'A' and the emotion of problematic envy. In problematic envy, your coachee either 'feels' deprived (non-ego problematic envy) or considers herself less worthy as a result of not having what the other has (ego problematic envy).

Aside from the emotional part of this response, when your coachee feels problematic envy, her behaviour will be dominated by a wish to make things even between herself and the other person, by getting what the other person has at all costs, by spoiling the other person's possession if she cannot get it or one like it for herself, or by denigrating the possession in some way. In addition, her subsequent thinking will exaggerate the importance of the possession and be dominated by plans to get the possession,

Table 7 Problematic jealousy vs. constructive jealousy
(concern for your relationship)

Adversity	• A threat is posed to your relationship with your partner from a third person • A threat is posed by uncertainty you face concerning your partner's whereabouts, behaviour or thinking in the context of the first threat	
Basic attitude	**RIGID AND EXTREME**	**FLEXIBLE AND NON-EXTREME**
Emotion	**Problematic jealousy**	**Constructive jealousy (concern for your relationship)**
Behaviour	• You seek constant reassurance that you are loved • You monitor the actions and feelings of your partner • You search for evidence that your partner is involved with someone else • You attempt to restrict the movements or activities of your partner • You set tests which your partner has to pass • You retaliate for your partner's presumed infidelity • You sulk	• You allow your partner to initiate expressing love for you without prompting him/her or seeking reassurance once he/she has done so • You allow your partner freedom without monitoring his/her feelings, actions and whereabouts • You allow your partner to show natural interest in members of the opposite sex without setting tests • You communicate your concern for your relationship in an open and non-blaming manner
Subsequent thinking	• You exaggerate any threat to your relationship that does exist • You think the loss of your relationship is imminent • You misconstrue your partner's ordinary conversations with relevant others as having romantic or sexual connotations • You construct visual images of your partner's infidelity • If your partner admits to finding another person attractive, you think that s/he finds that person more attractive than you and that s/he will leave you for this other person	• You tend not to exaggerate any threat to your relationship that does exist • You do not misconstrue ordinary conversations between your partner and other men/women • You do not construct visual images of your partner's infidelity • You accept that your partner will find others attractive but you do not see this as a threat

to spoil it or to denigrate it. It is important to note that the major motivation of your coachee's behaviour and thinking when she is unhealthily envious is to make things equal.

Constructive envy is, from an RECBT theoretical perspective, deemed to be the healthy alternative to problematic envy (for the final time, the important point here is the term you and your coachee have agreed to use as the healthy alternative to problematic envy). It stems from a set of flexible and non-extreme attitudes towards another person having something that your coachee prizes and desires but does not have. Aside from the emotional part of this response, when your coachee feels constructive envy, rather than problematic envy, she will be inclined, behaviourally, to pursue the possession, but only if she truly wants it. If she cannot get it, she will admire the possession without wanting to spoil it for the other or to denigrate it. Her subsequent thinking will be realistic and balanced in nature and locate the possession within an overall assessment of what the other person has and does not have in her life and what your coachee has and does not have in her life. As mentioned earlier, she will only make plans to get the possession if she really wants it and it will have enduring value for your coachee, and if the costs of pursuing the possession are not too great.

As with other emotions, your task is to help your coachee to develop a flexible and non-extreme attitude towards another person having something that your coachee prizes and desires but does not have, and to act and think in ways that are consistent with her flexible and non-extreme attitude. If she feels constructive envy rather than problematic envy, she will be able to come to terms with not having what the other has and to resume her coaching work towards her personal development objectives. Table 8 reviews, in full, the major features of problematic envy and constructive envy.

Having discussed the major factors involved in the eight main UNEs and their HNE alternatives, I will proceed to outline and

Table 8 Problematic envy vs. constructive envy

Adversity	• Another person possesses and enjoys something desirable that you do not have	
Basic attitude	**RIGID AND EXTREME**	**FLEXIBLE AND NON-EXTREME**
Emotion	**Problematic envy**	**Constructive envy**
Behaviour	• You disparage verbally the person who has the desired possession to others • You disparage verbally the desired possession to others • If you had the chance, you would take away the desired possession from the other (either so that you will have it or so that the other is deprived of it) • If you had the chance, you would spoil or destroy the desired possession so that the other person does not have it	• You strive to obtain the desired possession if it is truly what you want
Subsequent thinking	• You tend to denigrate in your mind the value of the desired possession and/or the person who possesses it • You try to convince yourself that you are happy with your possessions (although you are not) • You think about how to acquire the desired possession regardless of its usefulness • You think about how to deprive the other person of the desired possession • You think about how to spoil or destroy the other's desired possession • You think about all the other things the other has that you don't have	• You honestly admit to yourself that you desire the desired possession • You are honest with yourself if you are not happy with your possessions, rather than defensively trying to convince yourself that you are happy with them when you are not • You think about how to obtain the desired possession because you desire it for healthy reasons • You can allow the other person to have and enjoy the desired possession without denigrating that person or the possession • You think about what the other has and lacks and what you have and lack

discuss a step-by-step guide that you can use when you help your coachee deal with an emotional problem that she is bogged down with and which is serving as an obstacle to her pursuing her coaching-related personal development objectives because she cannot bypass the problem on her own sufficiently to concentrate on her coaching goals.

Notes

1 I made the point in Part 1 of this book that I will be using the term 'attitudes' rather than 'beliefs' to describe the evaluative cognitions at the heart of the RECBT model. To preserve the 'B' in the 'ABC' framework, when discussing it I use the term 'Basic' as a prefix to the term 'Attitudes'. The term 'Basic' here is designed to show that these attitudes are at the 'base' or the foundation of a person's response to adversity (see Dryden, 2016, for a fuller discussion of this point). This having been said, the terms 'Basic Attitudes' and 'Attitudes' are used interchangeably here.

2 It is important for you to note that I am talking about non-clinical depression here. Clinical depression is characterised by a number of biological features such as insomnia, loss of appetite, loss of libido and suicidal ideation. You should not attempt to help your coachee if she is experiencing this kind of depression. Rather, you should effect a referral to the coachee's general practitioner in the first instance.

3 If your coachee has a chronic problem with problematic jealousy, she probably requires ongoing therapy rather than time-limited focused help from you on this emotional problem. Only deal with an episode of problematic jealousy if your coachee does NOT have a chronic problem with this emotion.

Part 3

A step-by-step guide to dealing with your coachees' emotional problems

Introduction

In this part of the book, I will outline a step-by-step guide showing you how to deal with your coachee's emotional problem when it serves as an obstacle to her working towards her personal development objectives. In doing so, I will illustrate my points by referring to the case of Linda that I discussed earlier in the book

I have mentioned several times so far in this book that when your coachee experiences a problematic emotion about an adversity, this only serves as an obstacle to her pursuing her personal development objectives when she gets stuck in this unhealthy way of responding, cannot get out of it by herself and cannot bypass it sufficiently to focus on her personal development objectives. As such, you should only help her to address this emotional problem when she gets stuck and cannot bypass it on her own. If she initially experiences a problematic emotion in relation to an adversity but can respond productively to this emotion using her own existing resources, then let her do so and do not intervene. Indeed, if you make such an intervention, you might indicate to your coachee that she is not capable of dealing with such obstacles on her own when she has such capability.

Let me reiterate a point that I made in the Introduction to the book. Remember that your basic goal as a life coach is to help your coachee to identify, pursue and ultimately achieve her personal life objectives and not to help her with her emotional problems *per se* unless you are trained and sufficiently skilled to do so. Recall that the position that I take in this book is that you should only deal with your coachee's emotional problem when it serves as a specific obstacle to her pursuing her personal development objectives because she has become stuck in an unhealthy way of responding to the adversity and cannot bypass the problem sufficiently on her own to concentrate on her personal development objectives. If your coachee has many such emotional problems, then you should refer her to a psychotherapist or counsellor to deal with these emotional problems sufficiently so that she can then engage in coaching productively.

Having made this clear, let me stress that your first task is to assess whether or not your coachee has experienced a problematic emotion in relation to an adversity and has become bogged down in this emotion and cannot continue to pursue her personal development objectives because she is not able to bypass this emotional problem.

Step 1: Determine whether or not your coachee has an emotional problem; if she has, determine whether or not she is stuck and whether or not she can bypass it to pursue her personal development objectives

As you can see, there are three parts to this step:

- determining whether or not your coachee has an emotional problem

- determining whether or not she is stuck
- determining whether or not she is able to pursue her personal development objectives given that she is stuck with her emotional problem.

Determine whether or not your coachee has an emotional problem

In Part 2 of this book, I discussed the eight main problematic emotions that coachees experience when faced with life's adversities. These eight problematic emotions are: anxiety, depression, shame, guilt, hurt, problematic anger, problematic jealousy and problematic envy. In presenting these problematic emotions (which I referred to as unhealthy negative emotions or UNEs), I outlined the major behaviours (i.e. both overt actions and action tendencies) and the subsequent thinking that tend to accompany them. You should use this material as a guide in assessing whether or not your coachee has an emotional problem.

Case study: Does Linda have an emotional problem?

Throughout this part of the book, I will illustrate my points by referring to the work I did with Linda, who I was coaching because she was not feeling challenged in life. In our first two coaching sessions, I established where she needed to be challenged in life and we set a number of personal development objectives that she agreed to pursue before the next coaching session. Before I saw her next she learned that she failed to get a promotion that had been promised to her by her boss. Let me show you how I helped Linda and myself determine whether or not she had a problem about this. As I do so, I will comment on my inner dialogue as a coach and connect this with how I intervened with Linda. I will do this to help you understand the reasons for my interventions with Linda. Where appropriate I will use this inner dialogue to make more general points about how to use RECBT in similar situations.

WINDY: Since we last met what have you done to pursue your wish to get more challenge into your life?

LINDA: Well, I felt really inspired at the end of the last session. However, a few days later I found out from my boss that he was not going to promote me even though he had promised that he would do so.

WINDY: And how do you feel about this?

LINDA: Well, I felt and still feel really upset about it.

[Windy's observation: The term 'upset' is too vague for me to determine what type of emotion Linda is feeling and whether her emotional response is unhealthy or healthy. So I need to clarify this. I will do this by using her term 'upset' but linking it with more specific negative emotions.]

WINDY: Do you feel hurt upset, angry upset or…?

LINDA: Angry upset definitely.

[Windy's observation: OK, so now I know that Linda is angry, but I now need to find out whether this anger is healthy or not. I will start by looking at her behaviour.]

WINDY: When you feel angry, how do you express it?

LINDA: I don't.

[Windy's observation: Having drawn a blank here, I will now assess her action tendency, which is how she feels like expressing her anger but doesn't act on this feeling.]

WINDY: When you feel angry what do you feel like doing, but suppress?

LINDA: I feel like ripping him to shreds and giving him a real piece of my mind.

[Windy's observation: This seems very much like problematic anger, but I will double-check by assessing her associated thinking.]

WINDY: And how much do you think about this?

LINDA: It keeps going round and round in my mind. I can't seem to concentrate on anything else. So although I was planning to do a lot of preparatory work for this session, I just haven't had the mental space to do any.

[Windy's observation: Since angry rumination is a feature of problematic anger, this seems to confirm my hunch that Linda's anger is problematic for her. I will now ask her directly about this.]

WINDY: It's understandable that you feel angry about this, but anger can be problematic or constructive. While you don't express how you feel directly, you say that you feel like giving your boss a piece of your mind and ripping him to shreds. You also say that you are ruminating about this event a lot. Standing back for a moment, do you think that your anger is problematic or constructive for you?

LINDA: Put like that, I think it's really problematic.

Determine whether or not your coachee is stuck

As I mentioned earlier, the fact that your coachee has an emotional problem about an adversity does not justify you helping her with it within a coaching context. Many people experience emotional problems that temporarily derail them, but they are able to get to grips with them and move on and this may well be the case with your coachee. It is only when your coachee gets stuck or bogged down with the emotional problem and cannot move on in the pursuit of her personal development objectives, either by herself or with help from others, that she requires intervention from you. But how do you determine whether or not this is the case? Here are some suggestions. If your coachee has an emotional problem that has served as an obstacle to pursuing her personal development objectives, help her with this:

- if there has been no change in her feelings despite extended attempts at self-help
- if there has been no change in her feelings despite extended attempts at seeking informal help from others
- if she has no plans to deal with this emotional problem in the future and it is likely to continue
- if she cannot bypass this problem to refocus on her coaching-related personal development objectives (see next section).

Case study: Is Linda stuck?

WINDY: What have you tried to do to help yourself deal with your anger?

LINDA: Well, I have discussed what happened with my partner and friends, but they just seem to think that my anger is justified. My partner wants to confront my boss and 'punch his lights out'. I have tried punching a cushion and doing relaxation exercises, but nothing seems to help apart from in the very short term.

[Windy's observation: It seems that nothing Linda has tried has helped her to deal with her problematic anger. Let's see if she has any plans to deal with it more effectively.]

WINDY: Do you have any plans to deal with your anger?

LINDA: I was hoping that you might be able to help me in this respect.

[Windy's observation: Sounds like a specific invitation for me to intervene. But first I want to double-check to see if Linda's anger is an obstacle to her pursuing her personal development objectives.]

Determine whether or not being stuck with the emotional problem prevents your coachee from pursuing her personal development objectives

Although your coachee may be bogged down with her emotional problem, it does not follow that this will necessarily prevent her from pursuing the personal development objectives that she set with you earlier in the coaching process. Having said that, if she is stuck, then it is unlikely that she will have the mental space to detach from the problem and pursue her objectives. However, please note that I said 'unlikely' here and not 'impossible'. Some people are able to compartmentalise and pursue objectives in one area of their lives, while being emotionally bogged down in another area. So, even if you have a strong suspicion that your coachee will not be able to pursue her personal development objectives because she is stuck in dealing with her emotional problem, it is still important that you check this out with her in case you are wrong.

Case study: Is Linda's emotional problem an obstacle to her pursuing her personal development objectives?

WINDY: You said earlier that after our last session you felt inspired to put into practice what we discussed. Then, a few days later you found out that you were not going to get the promotion you were promised. Now, we have established that you feel problematically angry about this and we know that you feel stuck with your angry feelings. Is that right?

LINDA: That's correct.

[Windy's observation: Now I need to establish whether or not Linda is able to compartmentalise this problem and keep working towards her personal development objectives.]

WINDY: Have you been able to 'park' your angry feelings and keep working towards your personal development objectives or have they gotten in the way of you doing so?

LINDA: To be honest with you, I have let our work go because my mind has been on the promotion issue.

[Windy's observation: Finally, I'm going to assess whether or not Linda will be able to compartmentalise her angry feelings in the future.]

WINDY: And do you think that on your own you will be able to 'park' these feelings in the future and concentrate on our work together, or do you think you might want some help to deal with your problematic angry feelings?

LINDA: I don't think that I would know how to 'park' these feelings, as you call it. I would value some help.

Your coachee is stuck, but can compartmentalise and can work towards her personal development objectives: three ways forward

Now, what if your coachee can compartmentalise her emotional problem despite being stuck, and can keep working towards her personal development objectives? In such a case, you have three ways forward.

- You can keep helping your coachee to work towards her personal development objectives without helping her to deal with her emotional problem.

  In this case, you leave her to decide if and how she wants to tackle her emotional problem.
- You can keep helping her to work towards her personal development objectives and offer to help her get unstuck with respect to the emotional problem.

  In this case, recognise that you are moving into a counselling role with your coachee and thus your coaching contract with her may need to be renegotiated accordingly. You are moving into a counselling role here because you are departing from your coaching brief – which is to help your coachee reach her personal development objectives.
- You could keep helping her work towards her objectives and refer her to a counsellor who will help her with her emotional problem.

Whichever of these three options you choose will depend on (1) how you construe your role as a coach, and (2) the views of your coachee.

Please note that some coaches choose not to take on a counselling role and will therefore not take option 2 above, while others are happy to move from coaching to counselling and back again. In my experience, those in the latter group tend to be coaches who have previously trained as counsellors.

It is also important to note in this context that some coachees may have deliberately sought coaching even if they need counselling in some area of their lives. With such coachees, the very mention of counselling may put them off and spoil the working alliance that you have with them as a coach.

Case study: Discussing how we might deal with Linda's emotional problem

Having established that Linda had an emotional problem, was bogged down with it and could not compartmentalise it, I discussed with her how we might deal with this.

WINDY: OK, now there are a couple of possibilities here. First, I could help you with this emotional problem myself. This would involve me temporarily assuming a counselling role. Because it is temporary, doing so is not incompatible with my work as a coach. Second, I could refer you to a counselling colleague who will help you with this and when you are ready, we could resume our coaching work. What's your view?

LINDA: Well, if you can help me with this, I would like you to help me with the problem.

It is important to stress that any movement from coaching to counselling needs to be carefully explored with your coachee and explicitly agreed with her. This is definitely an issue that you should discuss with your coaching supervisor.

My final advice on this issue is for you to avoid switching from coaching to counselling with coachees who have particular difficulties handling situations where roles are ambiguous.

In proceeding with this book, let me stress that I shall be dealing with situations where a coachee:

- is working with you in coaching, has specified and is pursuing a set of personal development objectives
- has encountered an emotional problem that is interfering with her pursuing her personal development objectives
- has agreed to work with you to deal with this emotional problem so that she can resume the pursuit of her coaching goals.

Step 2: Elicit your coachee's explicit agreement to target this emotional problem for change and establish a contingency plan if you fail to help her

Developing a good working alliance between you and your coachee is an important ingredient of effective coaching (Bordin, 1979; Dryden, 2011, 2017). Such an alliance depends on (1) having a good bond between the two of you, (2) having a shared view of the coaching process, (3) agreeing on your coachee's personal development objectives, and (4) agreeing on what you and your coachee are going to do to help her achieve her objectives.

At this point in the coaching process you are deviating from your main role as a coach – which is to help your coachee to achieve her personal development objectives. Instead, you are adopting a temporary role of helping your coachee to remove the emotional obstacle that is preventing her from doing her work to achieve her personal development objectives. You may think, at this point, that you and your coachee have agreed to target for change her emotional problem, which is serving as an obstacle to her working towards her goal, but it is important that you explicitly do so. Some coaches prefer to document this agreement in writing. Whether or not you choose this more formal approach, my advice is to err on the side of caution and to reiterate this agreement and make it explicit. This is best done in a summary statement of what you and your coachee have discussed so far concerning the emotional obstacle to the pursuit of her personal development objectives.

In addition, you need to consider what you and your coachee are going to do if your attempts to help her with her emotional problems are not successful. Making a contingency plan for this eventuality at this stage is good ethical practice. What are your options here? You can do either of the following.

- Renegotiate your contract with your coachee from a coaching contract to a counselling contract. Effectively this means that you will help her with this problem more intensively and with any other emotional problems that she may have and refer her to another coach when she is ready to resume her pursuit of her personal development objectives.

- Refer her to a counsellor who will work with her on this emotional problem until she is ready to resume her coaching work with you.

Case study: Eliciting an agreement to target Linda's emotional problem for change

WINDY: So, Linda, let me summarise where we have got to so far. OK?

LINDA: OK.

WINDY: In our coaching work, we had identified your wish to be challenged more in life and you had been quite excited about beginning to identify how you might go about seeking such challenges. Then, your boss, who had promised to promote you, didn't do so. You responded with anger and we established that this anger is problematic in the sense that you have become stuck in your angry feelings and can't 'park' them sufficiently to keep focused on your coaching-related personal development objectives. Is that accurate?

LINDA: Very.

WINDY: We further considered how we were going to deal with this obstacle and we agreed that I was going to help you to deal with this problematic anger. Is that your understanding?

LINDA: Yes, it is.

Case study: Establishing a contingency plan with Linda

WINDY: OK, before we start, let's consider what happens if I can't help you with this obstacle. OK?

LINDA: OK.

WINDY: We need to establish a contingency plan to deal with this situation. I suggest that if this happens I refer you to one of my colleagues who is a counsellor and who would work with you more intensively to deal with this emotional problem. Then, when you are ready, we would resume our coaching work. How does that sound?

LINDA: Sounds good.

WINDY: OK, so let's go forward on that basis. OK?

LINDA: OK.

Step 3: Formulate the problem that is serving as an obstacle to the pursuit of your coachee's personal development objectives

When you focus on an emotional obstacle to the pursuit of your coachee's personal development objectives in the context of coaching, you will only be dealing with a single specific problem. Otherwise, you will be involved in counselling, not coaching.

You will have already established that your coachee has an emotional problem in Step 1. It is useful to summarise what you already know before proceeding.

Case study: Formulating the problem that is serving as an obstacle to Linda's pursuit of her personal development objectives

WINDY: Now we are focusing on your emotional problem, let me just review what you told me when we first talked about it. OK?

LINDA: OK.

WINDY: You made yourself angry about your boss not promoting you after telling you that he would. We discovered that your anger was problematic because

> you felt like ripping him to shreds and you were ruminating about the situation. Is that correct?
> *LINDA:* Yes, it is.

Formulate your coachee's emotional problem using the 'situational ABC' framework

When you help your coachee to formulate her emotional problem, you should have a clear statement of this problem informed by the 'situational ABC' framework that I discussed earlier in the book.

I suggest that you use the following points in formulating your coachee's emotional problem.

1. [**Situation**] – Help your coachee to identify the situation in which she experiences her problem.
2. [**'A'**] – 'A' is the aspect of the situation that your coachee was most disturbed about. It is not necessary to identify 'A' at this point since you will do so in Step 8.
3. [**'C' (emotional)**] – Help your coachee to identify the *one* major UNE that she experiences in the situation specified above. This will be one of the following: anxiety, depression, guilt, shame, hurt, problematic anger, problematic jealousy and problematic envy.
4. [**'C' (behavioural)**] – Help your coachee to identify the dysfunctional behaviour that your coachee demonstrated in this situation. Remember this might be an overt action or an action tendency.
5. [**'C' (cognitive)**] – If relevant, help your coachee to identify the thinking your coachee engaged in once her UNE 'kicked in'.
6. [**Effect on coaching goals**] – Help your coachee to specify the effect that this emotional problem has on their coaching goals (i.e. their personal development objectives).

Case study: Formalising Linda's formulated problem

Let me use my work with Linda and show how the above framework can be used.

1. Situation: *My boss told me that I would get promotion, but then he did not promote me.*
2. 'A': *Not known yet.*
3. 'C' (emotional): *Problematic anger.*
4. 'C' (behavioural): *Felt like ripping my boss to shreds.*
5. 'C' (cognitive): *Ruminating about not being promoted and what I would like to do to my boss.*
6. Effect on coaching goals: *This is stopping me from concentrating on and pursuing my personal development objectives.*

Putting this into a sentence, we have Linda's formulated problem.

> My boss told me that I would get promotion, but then he did not promote me. I feel unhealthily angry about this and feel like ripping my boss to shreds. I ruminate about doing so and about not being promoted. This is stopping me from concentrating on and pursuing my personal development objectives.

Step 4: Set a goal with respect to the formulated problem

It is useful at this point to help your coachee to set a goal with respect to her formulated problem (I will call this the 'target problem' in this book). Doing so gives your work on her emotional problem a sense of direction and helps your coachee to see that change is possible, which engenders a sense of hope and increases her motivation to engage in the process of RECBT.

Set your coachee's goal with respect to her formulated target problem using the 'situational ABC' framework

I suggest that you use the following points in helping your coachee to set a goal with respect to her formulated target emotional problem.

1. [Situation] – Help your coachee to identify the situation in which she experiences her problem. This will be the same as she specified in her formulated target problem.
2. ['A'] – Help your coachee to identify the theme of the problem. This will again be the same as your coachee specified in her formulated target problem. However, as mentioned above, it is not necessary for you to do this since you will do it in Step 8.
3. ['C' (emotional goal)] – Help your coachee to identify the healthy alternative to the major UNE that she experienced. Note that this emotional goal should be negative because it is about an adversity, but it should also be healthy in the sense that it will enable your coachee to deal effectively with the adversity if it can be changed or to adjust constructively to it if it cannot be changed. This will be one of the following: concern (as opposed to anxiety), sadness (as opposed to depression), remorse (as opposed to guilt), disappointment (as opposed to shame), sorrow (as opposed to hurt), constructive anger (as opposed to problematic anger), constructive jealousy (as opposed to problematic jealousy) and constructive envy (as opposed to problematic envy). It is important that you use your coachee's language when selecting an emotional goal and not necessarily the relevant term suggested by RECBT theory (Dryden, 1986).
4. ['C' (behavioural goal)] – Help your coachee to identify the functional alternative to the unconstructive behaviour that she demonstrated in her formulated target problem. Again this might be an overt action or an action tendency.

5. ['C' (cognitive goal)] – If relevant, help your coachee to identify the realistic alternative to the distorted thinking that she engaged in.

Note that when you help your coachee to set a goal for her formulated target problem, she is only changing her emotional, behavioural and thinking responses to the situation that she finds problematic. If she feels, acts and thinks in a healthy way in response to this situation, she is more likely to change the situation if it can be changed or adjust constructively and move on if it cannot be changed. Having a healthy set of responses will also help your coachee to refocus on and pursue her personal development objectives that you originally helped her to set in coaching.

Let me show how I used the above framework to help Linda set goals with respect to her emotional problem.

Case study: Setting a goal with Linda with respect to her formulated problem

WINDY: OK, Linda, let's see how you would like to handle the situation of being passed over for promotion by your boss. OK?

LINDA: OK.

WINDY: Well, we know that this situation happened so we can't do anything to prevent it from happening. Right?

LINDA: Well, I hope to get him to change his mind.

WINDY: Indeed, but you can't undo the past, can you?

LINDA: Sadly no.

WINDY: You mentioned you hope to get your boss to change his mind. Will your problematic anger and suppressing your wish to tear him to shreds help you to do this?

[Windy's observation: Here I am preparing the ground for setting goals by encouraging Linda to see the link between her problematic anger and her preferred outcome.]

LINDA: No, it won't.

WINDY: So would you be interested in a way of responding that reflects the negativity of your boss not keeping his promise to promote you, but enables you to assert yourself with him and also to resume your work towards your coaching goals without being preoccupied with the situation?

[Windy's observation: Here, I am suggesting that Linda considers a goal comprising what in RECBT we call a healthy negative emotion (HNE) and related behavioural and cognitive responses.]

LINDA: That sounds good.

WINDY: So I could help you feel healthily angry rather than unhealthily angry about your boss not promoting you. This would lead you to be assertive with him rather than wanting to rip him to shreds. Also, it would help you to get on with things with this in the back of your mind rather than ruminating on it. How does that sound?

[Windy's observation: In this intervention, I am explicitly contrasting problematic anger with constructive anger and their respective behavioural and cognitive responses.]

LINDA: Well, if you can help me do that, it would be great.

Case study: Formalising Linda's goals with respect to her formulated problem

Here, more formally, are the goals set by Linda whose emotional problem was formulated in Step 3. As noted above, the first two points are the same in the goal section as in the formulated problem section.

1. Situation: *My boss told me that I would get promotion, but then he did not promote me.*

2. 'A': *Not known yet.*
3. 'C' (emotional goal): *Constructive anger (rather than problematic anger).*
4. 'C' (behavioural): *Telling my boss that I was annoyed about this and asking him to explain his decision (rather than wanting to rip him to shreds).*
5. 'C' (cognitive): *Being aware of his decision, but getting on with things (rather than ruminating about it).*
6. Effect on coaching goals: *Being able to concentrate on and pursue my personal development objectives.*

Putting this into a few sentences, we have the coachee's goal with respect to her formulated target problem:

> My boss told me that I would get promotion, but then he did not promote me. I want to feel constructive anger (rather than problematic anger) about this and to tell him that I was annoyed about this and then ask him to explain his decision (rather than wanting to rip him to shreds). I want to be aware of his decision, but get on with things (rather than ruminating about it). Doing this will help me to concentrate on and pursue my personal development objectives.

Note that under the headings of 'emotional goal', 'behavioural goal' and 'cognitive goal', I suggest that you encourage your coachee to use 'rather than' wording to highlight the difference between her problem response and her goal response. However, if she finds doing this cumbersome, then suggest she omits the 'rather than' phrases.

Step 5: Assess for the presence of a meta-emotional problem and decide with the coachee if this is to become the target problem

When your coachee has an emotional problem, she may focus on this problem and disturb herself about it. Given this, it is important that you assess for the existence of what in RECBT is called her meta-emotional problem (literally an emotional problem about an emotional problem or a behavioural problem)

Thus, I suggest that you ask your coachee a question such as:

'How do you feel about......(state your coachee's original emotional/behavioural problem)?'

If your coachee does have a meta-emotional problem, you both need to decide if you need to deal with this before you focus on her original problem.

My advice is that you suggest to your coachee that you both focus on her original emotional/behavioural problem unless:

- the coachee wants to work on her meta-emotional problem first
- the existence of the coachee's meta-emotional problem will interfere with her focusing on her original emotional/behavioural problem in the session
- the existence of the coachee's meta-emotional problem will interfere with her working on her original emotional/behavioural problem in her life.

The important point is that you and your coachee agree on which of her problems (the original or her meta-emotional problem) to work on first. If you target her original problem and help her with this effectively, you may not need to help her with her meta-emotional problem if your coachee can resume work on her coaching goals without doing so.

Case study: Assessing for the presence of a meta-emotional problem and deciding with Linda if this is to become the target problem

Here is how I addressed this issue with Linda.

WINDY: OK. So you can see that your anger is problematic. Can you also see that constructive anger, where you feel like asserting yourself and in fact do assert yourself with your boss, and where you get on with life, mindful of the incident, but without rumination, is healthier for you?

LINDA: Yes.

WINDY: Before we get down to the business of helping you, I just want to bring up one issue. Now, when you experience problematic anger and you focus on that anger, how do you feel about your angry feelings?

LINDA: Well...I'm not sure what you mean.

WINDY: OK. For example, do you feel ashamed of feeling that way, or anxious...?

LINDA: Oh, I see. No. I am too busy feeling angry...

WINDY: What about when you calm down and focus on your anger then?

[Windy's observation: This is an important point. Your coachees may disturb themselves about their UNE either at the time or later when they are not in the grip of such feelings. It is worth asking about both possibilities.]

LINDA: No, if anything I feel justified in how I feel...But, now I can see that there is the possibility of feeling and reacting with constructive anger, I guess I can feel justified in feeling anger and still be healthy.

[Windy's observation: Linda raises a number of important points here. First, your coachee may well construe their UNE positively and this needs to be tackled if it persists later in the process. Second, your coachee may change her mind about the perceived benefit of her UNE when she understands and commits herself to the healthy alternative to this UNE (i.e. her HNE).]

WINDY: Good point. So as you don't have what we call a meta-emotional problem, literally an emotional problem about your problematic anger, we can proceed to helping you deal with your problematic anger.

Step 6: Ask for a concrete example of the coachee's formulated target problem

Once you have helped your coachee to formulate her target problem and set a related goal, I suggest that you help her to select a concrete example of this problem. Working with a concrete example will provide you both with specific information about your coachee's 'A' and 'C', which will help you to identify a specific rigid and extreme attitude at 'B'. If your coachee's problem is specific enough anyway, then you may skip this step. If not, ask your coachee:

'Can you give me a concrete example of this problem?'

A concrete example is one that occurred in a specific situation at a specific time in the presence of a specific person or persons.

If your coachee finds it difficult to select a concrete example of her target problem, you can suggest that she pick an example that is fresh in her mind. This example might be:

- recent
- vivid
- typical
- future.

It may seem strange to talk about a future example of the coachee's problem, but if you think about it, it is not so strange. Your coachee may imagine a future scenario and when she does so, she may disturb herself about it because she brings to that future event a disturbance-creating rigid and extreme attitude. In what follows, Linda selects a future example of her emotional problem and you will see how I handled this.

Case study: Asking for a concrete example of Linda's formulated target problem

WINDY: So now let's discuss your problematic anger. It would be useful if you could pick a specific example of your anger problem with your boss. This might be something that has happened, is happening or you anticipate happening.

LINDA: Well, I would like to talk to him about it, but I think if I do I will lose my temper.

WINDY: So, let's focus on that. Can you tell me about the specific situation you envisage?

[Windy's observation: As Linda has chosen a future specific example, I need to get as much detail as I can about the likely context.]

LINDA: Well, it would be in his office just before lunch and I would have asked to see him about not being promoted.

[Windy's observation: This is sufficient detail to go on to the next step.]

Step 7: Identify 'C'

At this point you may well know the specific emotion that your coachee experienced in the concrete example that she has selected for assessment. After all, you will have formulated her emotional problem and the relevant unhealthy negative emotion (UNE) should have been made explicit in this formulation. However, there may be times when the UNE has not been specified in this formulation and it is only when your coachee discusses a specific example of her emotional problem that the relevant UNE becomes clear.

As you will remember, 'C' stands for the consequences of your coachee's rigid and extreme attitudes towards 'A'. 'C' can be emotional, behavioural and cognitive. It is important at this point that you assess your coachee's major UNE in the selected example. If she experiences several, help her to select the main one. Additionally, if you can also identify the associated behaviour that would be good. Identifying the subsequent thinking is, in my opinion, optional if you have assessed the emotional and behavioural aspects of 'C', but it may be important, particularly if your coachee gets caught up in such thinking as in rumination.

You might be thinking, why begin with 'C'? Why not start with 'A'? In my view, if you start with 'C' and, in particular, your coachee's major UNE, this emotion helps you to identify her 'A' by giving you clues concerning the likely theme of the 'A'. For example, if your coachee says that she feels anxious, you know that the theme of 'threat' is likely to be present in her 'A'. I refer you to the material I outlined in Part 2 of this book where I discussed the main cognitive-behavioural features of the eight UNEs and their HNE alternatives. As I said earlier, 'C' can be behavioural, cognitive as well as emotional, but I suggest that you start with the emotional 'C' since this is the component that will most aid you in then assessing your coachee's 'A'.

Start with the emotional 'C'

Ask the coachee to identify how she felt in the situation in question. Help her to select one UNE and, if she felt several, help her to identify the main one. Thus, you can ask:

'How did you feel when…(state the situation)…?'

When all goes well, your coachee will clearly state that her emotional 'C' is both negative and unhealthy. However, the course of RECBT, like the course of true love, rarely runs smoothly and if you encounter the following, here is what I suggest you do.

Your coachee's emotional 'C' is vague

Here, your coachee may say that she 'feels' bad or upset. Such expressions of negative emotion are unclear and, when stated thus, you do not know what your coachee's negative emotional 'C' is, nor do you know if it is unhealthy or healthy. When this happens, it is important that you help your coachee to be more specific about her feelings.

For example:

COACH: How did you feel when your dad quickly passed you on to your mum when you phoned home?
COACHEE: I felt bad.
COACH: I am not sure what emotion that refers to. Can you be more specific?
COACHEE: I felt hurt.

You are not sure if your coachee's negative 'C' is healthy or unhealthy

While RECBT theory is clear in its language when differentiating between UNEs and HNEs (see Tables 1–8), your coachee is unlikely to use the same language when referring to her emotions. Thus, your coachee may give you an emotion that sounds like a UNE, but you are not sure whether it is or not. Alternatively, in response to your request to be specific about her negative emotion, your coachee may continue to be vague about her feelings.

What can you do in such circumstances? If you look at Tables 1–8, you will see that, apart from the different names given to unhealthy and healthy negative emotion pairs, each emotion within a pairing (e.g. anxiety and concern) is associated with different behaviours (i.e. overt actions and action tendencies) and different subsequent thinking. Given this, it is possible for you to infer your coachee's emotion by discovering how she acted in the situation that you are assessing and/or how she thought after her feelings had 'kicked in'. Let me show you what I mean by revisiting the example above.

> COACH: How did you feel when your dad quickly passed you on to your mum when you phoned home?
>
> COACHEE: I felt bad.
>
> COACH: I am not sure what emotion that refers to. Can you be more specific?
>
> COACHEE: I am not sure that I can.
>
> COACH: OK. When you felt bad about your dad quickly passing you on to your mum when you phoned, what did you do or feel like doing?
>
> COACHEE: I felt like putting the phone down.
>
> COACH: Why?
>
> COACHEE: Because I felt that my dad always does this to me and wouldn't do that if it was my sister who rang.
>
> COACH: Could you tell your dad how you feel at that point?
>
> COACHEE: No.
>
> COACH: Why not?
>
> COACHEE: Because I don't feel like talking to him when he does that. I just want to go into my shell and make him suffer.
>
> COACH: So, correct me if I am wrong but my sense is that you felt hurt when your father quickly passed the phone on to your mother? Is that right?
>
> COACHEE: Very much so. I did feel hurt.

By utilising the information provided in Tables 1–8 and matching it to what his coachee said about how she felt like acting (i.e. her action tendency) and how she thought in the situation when she felt 'bad', the coach hypothesised that his coachee's 'C' was hurt, a hunch that was confirmed by his coachee.

Your coachee's stated emotional 'C' is really an inference

As I discussed earlier in the book, when your coachee's emotional problem serves as an impediment to the coaching work that you are doing together in the service of her personal development objectives, she is likely to experience a major UNE such as: anxiety, depression, guilt, shame, hurt, problematic anger, problematic jealousy, problematic envy. She may experience more than one such emotion and, if so, you need to deal with one emotion at a time.

Having said this, when you ask your coachee what emotion she experienced in the specific example of her emotional problem, she may not give you one of the above listed emotions. Apart from being vague about her feelings (which I discussed above), your coachee may say that her emotion is really an inference when you ask her for her emotional 'C'. An inference is an interpretation that your coachee made about the situation that she was in that was related to her emotional response but which went beyond the data at hand. Your coachee may have been correct in making her inference or she may have been incorrect. However, she may think that her inference was factual. Actually, these 'inferences as emotions' frequently turn out to be your coachee's 'As'.

Here are some examples of inferences that coachees mistake for emotions:

- 'I felt rejected.'
- 'I felt criticised.'
- 'I felt attacked.'
- 'I felt wronged.'

As you can see, none of the above represent a coachee's emotional 'C'. They are inferences. For example, when your coachee says that she 'felt wronged', she means that the person in the specific example of her emotional problem that she has chosen acted in a way that transgressed one of your coachee's rules. It is highly probable that your coachee experienced an emotion about 'being wronged' and, if you have done your work well up to this point, it is likely that this emotion is a UNE (i.e. negative and unhealthy). But what is important to note is that your coachee has not been explicit about this emotional 'C'. It is your job to help your coachee to do this. Here are some examples of how to do so.

The 'about' method. Here is what you do when you use the 'about' method. When your coachee provides you with an inference instead of an emotion in response to your enquiry about her emotional 'C', you treat her response as an inference and ask the coachee how she felt *about* this inference.

> COACH: How did you feel when your boss gave you feedback about your report?
> COACHEE: I felt criticised.
> COACH: Do you mean that your boss was criticising you or just your report?

[Windy's observation: Here the coach seeks to clarify whether the criticism referred to criticism of her work or criticism of her entire self. The latter proved to be the case.]

> COACHEE: I thought he was criticising me as a person.
> COACH: And when you thought that your boss was criticising you as a person, how did you feel *about* his criticism?
> COACHEE: I felt hurt about that.

Caution. When your coachee gives you an inference when you have asked for her emotional 'C' and this inference is clearly distorted, you may well be tempted to focus on this inference with a view to encouraging your coachee to question it. It is important to resist this temptation for two reasons. First, your task at this point is to help your coachee to identify her emotional 'C' in the specific example of her emotional problem that she has selected. If you switch to questioning her inference, then you are not going to identify this emotional 'C'. Second, when you help your coachee to question her inference without identifying her underlying rigid and extreme attitudes and helping her to question and change them, then you are not helping her as fully as you can. In RECBT we say that since your coachees' emotional problems are largely determined by their rigid and extreme attitudes, rather than their distorted inferences, then the best way of helping them with emotional problems is to help them to develop a healthier set of flexible and non-extreme attitude alternatives rather than a set of realistic inferences. The problem with encouraging your coachee to make an inferential change rather than an attitude-based change is that the relief (albeit short term) that she gets from changing her inference will lessen her motivation to change her rigid and extreme attitude.

In summary, when your coachee gives you an inference instead of an emotion at this juncture, remember to use the inference to identify the emotional 'C' and resist the temptation to question the inference.

Ask for behavioural and/or thinking 'Cs' and infer the emotional 'C'

If for any reason your coachee continues to struggle to give you an emotional 'C', then you can temporarily bypass this and infer the emotion from her behaviour (overt action and action tendency) or her subsequent thinking. Before doing so, I suggest that you familiarise yourself with Tables 1–8 in Part 2 of this book.

What you do is this:

• Ask your coachee to imagine that she is in the situation that she selected in which she experienced her emotional problem.

- Assess how she acted in this situation or what she felt like doing, but did not do.
- If necessary, ask her what thoughts she had after her 'yet to be identified' feelings had 'kicked in'.
- Form a hypothesis concerning what your coachee's emotional 'C' could have been given her behavioural 'C' and/or thinking 'C'.
- Ask your coachee to consider this.

Here is an example of this approach in practice.

> COACH: So how did you feel when you discovered that your friend had divulged your confidence to another mutual friend?
>
> COACHEE: I felt bad about it.
>
> COACH: Can you clarify that emotion a bit more?
>
> COACHEE: I am not sure that I can.
>
> COACH: OK, is it alright if I ask you a number of specific questions that will help both of us discover the nature of your emotion?
>
> COACHEE: OK.
>
> COACH: Great. Cast your mind back to when you first discovered that your friend had divulged your confidence to another common friend. What did you do?
>
> COACHEE: Well I bitched about it to my friends.

[Windy's observation: This doesn't really help the coach. He needs to focus his coachee's attention on how she behaved to her friend or on what she felt like doing, but did not actually do.]

> COACH: OK, what did you do to your friend who betrayed your trust in this way?
>
> COACHEE: I didn't do anything.
>
> COACH: Did you feel an urge to say or do something to your friend that in the end you suppressed?

COACHEE: Funny you should ask that, because I did have to suppress an urge to do something to her.
COACH: And what was that urge?
COACHEE: Well, I wanted to sulk and not talk to her and to spread some nasty gossip about her.

[Windy's observation: The coachee is giving clues that she felt either angry about her friend's behaviour or hurt about it.]

COACH: So by the sound of it you felt either problematic anger or hurt.
COACHEE: Well, I think it was both of those feelings. I mainly felt hurt though.

So, in this example, the coachee revealed in response to the coach's specific line of questioning that she felt both hurt and problematic anger, but that her hurt was her main UNE.

Case study: Identifying Linda's C

You will recall that when I asked Linda for a specific example of her anger problem, she chose a future example where she would be in her boss's office just before lunch having asked to see him about not being promoted. This is how I identified her emotional 'C' in this situation.

WINDY: So how do you think you will feel in your boss's office just before lunch having asked to see him about not being promoted?
LINDA: I would feel angry.

[Windy's observation: Although Linda's formulated problem is problematic anger, I am not going to assume that her anger in the specific example she has chosen is necessarily

---

unhealthy. I need to get evidence before concluding that it is and helping Linda to see this.]

WINDY: Your anger could be constructive or problematic and I would like to clarify which it is if that is OK?
LINDA: That's fine.
WINDY: When you anticipate feeling angry, what would you feel like doing at that moment?
LINDA: I wouldn't do this, of course, but I would feel like shouting abuse at him and giving him a slap.
WINDY: Now does that sound like constructive anger to you?
LINDA (laughing): Certainly not!

Step 8: Identify 'A'

While you are assessing 'A', it is important for you to remember that 'A' is the most relevant part of the situation that triggered your coachee's rigid and extreme attitude at 'B', which, in turn, largely determined her UNE at 'C'.

The standard question in assessing 'A'

When you assess 'A', here is the most common way of doing so. Ask:

'What were you most......about (state the coachee's 'C') when......(state the situation)?'

If I was using this question with Linda, I would ask:

'What do you think you will be most unhealthily angry about when you see your boss in his office to talk about why you were not promoted?'

Windy's Magic Question

Here is another method, which I call 'Windy's Magic Question', if the above question does not yield the 'A'.

- Focus on the 'situation' that your coachee has described.
- Ask her what one thing would get rid of or significantly diminish the UNE that she felt at 'C'.
- The opposite to this is, most probably, your coachee's 'A'.

Case study: Linda

Here is how I would have used this method with Linda.

Her described 'situation' is: 'Going to see my boss in his office at lunchtime to talk about me not being promoted' and her emotional 'C' was problematic anger.

- Focus your coachee's attention on the 'situation' that she described: *'Going to see my boss in his office at lunchtime to talk about me not being promoted.'*
- Ask her what one thing would get rid of or significantly diminish the anxiety that she felt at 'C': *'That my boss had not broken his promise to me.'*
- The opposite of this is your coachee's 'A': *'My boss broke his promise to me.'*

Encourage your coachee to assume temporarily that 'A' is true

When you assess 'A', you may discover that your coachee's 'A' is a clear distortion of reality. If this is the case, you may be tempted to question 'A'. As I discussed in the previous step, it is important that you resist this temptation. Rather, at this stage you should encourage your coachee to assume temporarily that 'A' is correct.

For example, in the case previously described, it is not important to determine whether your coachee's boss has broken his promise to her. What is important is that you encourage your coachee to assume that 'A' is correct in order to help her to identify more accurately the rigid and extreme attitudes towards the 'A' that led to her feelings at 'C'. Later, you will have an opportunity to check whether 'A' is likely to have been true (see Step 21).

There may be times when your coachee will want to question 'A' and not want to go on to identify her rigid and extreme attitudes at 'B'. I suggest that you go along with this, but only after you have made several attempts to show her the importance of identifying rigid and extreme attitudes. If these fail, not questioning 'A' at this point would threaten the working alliance you have with your coachee. If you need to question 'A' at this point, proceed straight to Step 21.

Avoid pitfalls in assessing 'A'

There are a number of pitfalls in assessing 'A'. The following suggestions can help you to avoid them.

1. Do not obtain too much detail about the situation in which the coachee's 'A' is embedded. Allowing your coachee to talk at length about the situation can discourage you both from retaining a problem-solving approach to overcoming her emotional problems. If your coachee does provide too much detail, try to abstract the salient theme or summarise what you understand to be her 'A'. Interrupt your coachee tactfully and re-establish an RECBT-driven assessment focus if she does begin to discuss the situation at length. For example, you could say, 'I think you may be giving me more detail than I require. What was it about the situation that you were most disturbed about?'

2. Do not assume that the first inference that your coachee comes up with is her 'A'. Ask for other inferences that she might have made in the situation, then apply 'Windy's Magic Question' (see above) to identify your coachee's 'A'.

3. Do not accept an 'A' unless it reflects the theme associated with the UNE you have already assessed. Consult Tables 1–8 in Part 2 of this book for information about inferential themes associated with the eight emotional problems for which coachees typically seek help.

Case study: Identifying Linda's 'A'

Here is how I identified Linda's 'A'.

WINDY: So what do you think you will be most angry about when you go to see your boss to discuss not being promoted?

LINDA: Well, he said he would promote me and then he didn't do so.

WINDY: So apart from giving you promotion, what could you discover at the meeting that would eliminate or significantly reduce your problematic anger?

[Windy's observation: This is a version of 'Windy's Magic Question' technique explained above.]

LINDA: Well, I am pretty sure that he will try to wriggle out of it, but I think that if he convinced me that he hadn't broken his promise to me, then that would definitely help.

WINDY: So would I be correct in assuming, then, that you would be most problematically angry about your boss breaking his promise to you and not promoting you when he said he would?

> *LINDA:* Absolutely. I really do have a thing about broken promises.

Step 9: Elicit your coachee's emotional goal in the specific example being assessed

It is important that your work as a coach is forward looking and this means that you will encourage your coachee to set personal development objectives that give the coaching work a positive direction. When dealing with your coachee's emotional problem obstacle to the pursuit of her personal development objectives, there are two places that you will want to set goals which also give this 'overcoming obstacles' work a forward-looking thrust. I have already discussed the first place in Step 4 when I showed you how you can help your coachee to set a goal with respect to her formulated target problem. The second place is here after you have assessed the 'A' and 'C' elements of your coachee's selected specific example of her formulated problem.

Thinking about your coachee's goal in the specific example under consideration

Before eliciting your coachee's goal with respect to her selected specific example, it is important to compare what you mean by this and what your coachee might mean by it. In RECBT, when we think about a coachee's goals concerning a specific example of her target emotional problem, we think in terms of the situation and the 'A' remaining constant with the coachee responding differently at 'C'. However, your coachee may have a very different idea about her goal. Let me take Linda as an example here and demonstrate what I mean. First, I will outline the 'ABC' of the specific example of Linda's problem.

Case study: Linda

Problem	Goal
Situation	**Situation**
Going to see my boss in his office at lunchtime to talk about me not being promoted	Going to see my boss in his office at lunchtime to talk about me not being promoted
'A'	**'A'**
My boss broke his promise to me	My boss broke his promise to me
'B'	**'B'**
Not yet assessed	Not yet assessed
'C'	**'C'**
Emotional 'C': Problematic anger	Emotional 'C' goal: Alternative emotion (negative and healthy)
Behavioural 'C': Feeling like shouting abuse at him and giving him a slap	Behavioural 'C' goal: Alternative overt behaviour or action tendency (constructive)

Now, imagine that when I asked Linda what her goal would be with respect to her response in the forthcoming meeting with her boss, she said: 'To get my boss to change his mind and keep his promise to promote me.' I will call this her 'hypothetical response' in which she points to two things:

- an allusion to her behaviour, although it is not clear what this behaviour is
- a change in the behaviour of her boss.

In reality, I helped Linda to set a goal that was in her power to achieve, which I will call her 'actual response', as shown below.

1   Situation: *Going to see my boss in his office at lunchtime to talk about me not being promoted.*
2   'A': *My boss broke his promise to me.*
3   'B': *Not yet assessed.*

4   'C' (emotional): *Constructive anger.*
5   'C' (behavioural): *Asserting myself to my boss and advancing cogent reasons for my promotion.*

Let me now compare her actual response with her hypo-thetical response (i.e. 'To get my boss to change his mind and keep his promise to promote me') – see Table 9.

You will see from this table that in her hypothetical response:

• Linda did not set a clear HNE as an emotional goal. In fact she did not mention an emotional goal at all.
• Linda was unclear about her behavioural goal.
• Linda set as a goal a change in another person.

You will further see from Table 9 that in her actual response:

• Linda did set a clear HNE as an emotional goal.
• Linda was clear about her behavioural goal.
• Linda did not set as a goal a change in another person.

Table 9 Linda's actual and hypothetical responses when asked for a goal concerning her selected specific example

	Actual Response	Hypothetical Response
Clear HNE Specified	Yes	No
Specific Constructive Behaviour Specified	Yes	No
Change in Another Person Specified	No	Yes

HNE = Healthy Negative Emotion

Summary of dos and don'ts when eliciting your coachee's problem-related goal

In summary, when eliciting your coachee's goal with respect to her response to the situation in which her emotional problem occurred or is likely to occur, you should ideally follow these dos and don'ts:

- Do help your coachee to specify an HNE in response to the situation in which the adversity at 'A' occurred (or is likely to occur).
- Do help your coachee to specify a constructive behavioural response to this 'A'.
- Don't help your coachee to set goals that are outside her direct control (e.g. a change in the behaviour of another person).

Help your coachee to understand that changing her emotional 'C' will increase her chances of bringing about a change in 'A' if it can be changed

When you attempt to elicit a goal from your coachee with respect to her selected specific example of her target problem, you may find that your coachee will cling doggedly to the wish to change the adversity at 'A'. If this happens, what can you do? I will focus here on the situation where your coachee wishes to change the behaviour of another person involved in the specific example.

Help your coachee to see the difference between changing another person and influencing that person

Help your coachee to see that there is a difference between changing another person and influencing that person. Help your coachee to understand that were you to accept the goal of changing the other person, you would be encouraging your coachee to change what is outside her direct control to change. Rather, help her to see that the other person's behaviour is under their direct control and not your coachee's.

If your coachee accepts this, show her that it does not mean there is nothing that she can do. Show her that she can influence that person to change and that as these attempts to influence the other person are under your coachee's direct control, they are acceptable as behavioural goals.

Help your coachee to understand that influencing another person is best done when she is not emotionally disturbed

Once your coachee has set 'attempts to influence the other person' as her behavioural goal, ask her whether her influence behaviours are more likely to be successful if she is in an emotionally disturbed frame of mind or if she is in an emotionally healthy frame of mind. Most coachees can see that being in an emotionally healthy frame of mind will increase their chances of persuading the other person to change – without, of course, guaranteeing this outcome.

Case study: Eliciting Linda's emotional goal in the specific example being assessed

Here is how I responded to Linda in this goal-eliciting step when she continued to express a desire to get her boss to change his mind and promote her.

WINDY: So, instead of feeling unhealthily angry and feeling like shouting abuse at him and giving him a slap, what is your goal in this situation?
LINDA: To get him to change his mind.

[Windy's observation: Linda is focused on changing her boss rather than changing her responses, so let me address this issue.]

WINDY: Who is ultimately in charge of your boss's decision to promote you: him or you?

LINDA: Sadly, him.

WINDY: What are you in charge of with respect to, as you put it, 'getting him to change his mind'?

LINDA: I guess my own behaviour.

WINDY: You guessed right!...(both laugh)...So is feeling like shouting abuse at him and giving him a slap a good foundation for increasing the chances of influencing him to promote you?

LINDA (laughs): No.

WINDY: And what alternative behaviour would increase your chances?

LINDA: Being assertive with him and coming up with rational arguments as to why he should keep his promise to promote me.

WINDY: And will your feelings of problematic anger help you or hinder you in this respect?

LINDA: It will hinder me...definitely.

WINDY: So you need a feeling that acknowledges the badness of your boss's broken promise to you and that helps you to assert yourself and give those rational arguments. Would you want to set that as your feeling goal?

LINDA: Sounds good.

WINDY: So what would you call that emotion? Remember it needs to be negative and acknowledge the badness of the broken promise, but it also needs to help you to be assertive and give rational arguments.

LINDA: I would like to call it constructive anger.

WINDY: Rather than unhealthy anger?

LINDA: Yes.

[Windy's observation: It is important to use a coachee's language when referring to an HNE goal. Constructive annoyance is close enough to constructive anger to be acceptable, in my view.]

> *WINDY:* So let me sum up. Rather than feel unhealthily angry with your boss for breaking his promise to you, you have set as your goal to feel constructively angry about the broken promise instead. While problematic anger leads you to want to shout abuse at your boss and slap him, an urge which fortunately you are able to suppress, constructive anger would help you to actually assert yourself with him and allow you to provide rational arguments as to why he should change his mind back and keep his promise. However, you also recognise that all you can do is to control your own behaviour and you recognise that no matter how persuasive you may be, in the final analysis your boss is in charge of whether or not he chooses to promote you. Is that summary accurate?
>
> *LINDA:* Very accurate.

Ways of eliciting an emotional goal

In coaching as in life, what you get is largely determined by how you go about trying to get it. This is especially true when it comes to eliciting your coachee's emotional goal. Let me review such strategies.

Ask for a goal in an open-ended way

When you ask your coachee for an emotional goal, you simply refer to her goal without qualifying this in any way. Examples of such an approach are:

- What would like to achieve in discussing this example with me?
- What is your goal here?

These are open-ended questions and while they give your coachee freedom to express her goal in her own way, they are problematic in that such questions decrease the chances of you getting what you are looking for: an emotional response (to the adversity at 'A') that is negative and healthy and as such is a constructive alternative to your coachee's actual emotional response, which is both negative and unhealthy.

In outlining goal statements in response to the open-ended question, I will briefly comment on the problems with them and how to address them.

Thus, in response to such open-ended questions your coachee may say that she wants the following.

To change the other person. I have discussed the issues relevant to this on pp. 91–92.

To be indifferent to the adversity (in other words to have a neutral emotion). Here Linda might say: 'My goal is not to care about not being promoted.'

This is only possible if Linda truly did not care about not being promoted, but she does care and helping her to achieve the goal of indifference would be encouraging her to lie to herself. Help your coachee to see this and that she needs to commit herself to feeling an emotion that reflects the fact that she does care about not getting what she wants, for example, but that does not reflect emotional disturbance.

To change her own behaviour in a constructive way without mentioning a change in emotion. Here, Linda might say: 'I want to assert myself with my boss.'

Help your coachee to see that her constructive behaviour is linked with an HNE. Help her to formulate this and give it a name that makes sense to her.

To change the situation. Here Linda might say: 'I want to find another job.'

The trouble with this goal is that it is not focused on a healthy emotional response and thus is likely to be based on the same rigid and extreme attitude that underpins her emotional problem in the first place. Help your coachee to see that such decisions are best taken when she is in a healthy frame of mind and for this to be achieved she needs to deal with her emotional problem, not bypass the problem or take a decision that is, in fact, based on the problem. As such, proceed to help her to set a healthy emotional goal in response to her adversity at 'A'.

To change her own behaviour but in an unconstructive way. Here, Linda might say: 'I want to get back at my boss without him finding out about it.'

When your coachee comes up with a goal that is unconstructive, she may not initially realise that it is so. Thus, your first step is to help her to see that the goal is unconstructive. In Linda's case her behavioural goal (as stated above) is an expression of her problematic anger, not a healthy alternative to it. After your coachee understands the dysfunctionality of her behavioural goal, then you can begin to help her to construct a healthy one.

Ask for an emotional goal

When you ask your coachee for an emotional goal in the specific example, you are asking her to specify an emotion that she could have experienced that is different from the emotion that she did experience. Examples of such an approach are:

- How would you have liked to have felt in this situation?
- What would have been a more healthy emotion for you to have experienced in this situation?

Desired versus healthy emotional goals. Note the differences between the above two questions. The first asks the coachee to give her preference for an alternative emotion, while the second asks her to think about the healthiness of the alternative emotion. Both have their problems. In the first, the coachee may wish to experience an emotion that is not healthy, while, in the second, the coachee may be able to specify a healthy emotional alternative, but not wish to experience it.

It follows, therefore, that if you ask for an emotional goal in response to the adversity at 'A', you need to ensure (1) that the coachee can specify an HNE that is a good alternative to the UNE she experienced in the specific example of her emotional problem, and (2) that she wants to experience this emotion.

Seeking less of a disturbed emotion. When you ask your coachee for her emotional goal in the selected specific example, in addition to her wanting to feel indifference or calm in the face of adversity (see above), she may opt to feel less of the disturbed emotion in question. On the face of it, this may seem quite reasonable. Thus, for example, if your coachee experiences strong anxiety in her selected specific example, what is wrong with her wanting to feel less of this painful emotion?

RECBT's position on the difference between UNEs and HNEs is that the former stem from rigid and extreme attitudes and the latter stem from flexible and non-extreme attitudes (see Tables 1–8). As rigid and extreme attitudes are *qualitatively* rather than *quantitatively* different from flexible and non-extreme attitudes (i.e. meaning they are on different continua, not at the opposite ends of the same continuum), it follows that UNEs are qualitatively, not quantitatively, different from HNEs. Thus, an HNE is on a different continuum from its UNE counterpart and not on opposite ends of the same continuum.

Since an HNE has its own continuum, its health is not determined by its intensity but by the fact that it is underpinned by flexible and non-extreme attitudes, as I discussed earlier in the book (see pp. 27–28). Thus, an HNE can be strong and healthy.

It follows from the above that if your coachee wants to feel less of a disturbed emotion, she will still be experiencing a disturbed emotion. If you accept this as a legitimate emotional goal, what you will, in effect, be doing is helping your coachee to strive to acquire a weaker version of the rigid and extreme attitudes that underpin her more intense UNE.

If your coachee does specify a less intense version of her UNE as her goal, you need to do the following.

1. Help her to see that a less intense disturbed emotion is still a disturbed emotion and is still linked to unconstructive overt behaviours and action tendencies.
2. Help her to set more constructive behavioural responses.
3. Help her to see that an HNE alternative to her UNE is associated with these constructive behavioural responses and that it can remain healthy even if it is a strong emotion.
4. Have her name the HNE and use this name subsequently in your work with her.

Eliciting an emotional goal based on an explanation of what you are looking for

So far I have discussed two strategies for eliciting your coachee's emotional goal in the selected specific example that were based on asking questions [(1) for a goal and (2) for an emotional goal]. In using both types of questions, you are not being clear about what you are looking for and thus both are problematic and can lead you to deal with issues that you may not have had to deal with if you were clear about what you are looking for. Given this, I recommend that you use a strategy to elicit an emotional goal that is based more on explaining what you are looking for and why you are looking for it. As such, this strategy is more theory-driven than the two questioning strategies in that it is derived directly from the theory of RECBT concerning the difference between UNEs and HNEs.

Case study: Linda

Here is how I suggest using this explanation-based strategy. In doing so, I will show you how I would have used this strategy with Linda.

1. Review what you have already identified with respect to your coachee's specific example and write the resulting

'situational ABC' on a whiteboard under the heading 'Problem' to remind your coachee that this 'situational ABC' relates to a specific example of her emotional problem. Thus, with Linda I would have written the following.

Problem

Situation
Going to see my boss in his office at lunchtime to talk about me not being promoted

'A'
My boss broke his promise to me

'B'
Not yet assessed

'C'
Emotional 'C': Problematic anger
Behavioural 'C': Feeling like shouting abuse at him and giving him a slap

---

2. Explain that the situation is not going to change. In Linda's case, the reality is that she is going into the boss's office at lunchtime to discuss with him the fact that she was not promoted.

3. Encourage her to continue to assume temporarily that her 'A' was correct since she was reacting to it as though it were true in the specific example of her emotional problem and thus, if she is to respond to it more constructively, she needs to continue to assume 'A' is true, albeit again temporarily. In Linda's case I would have encouraged her to continue to assume that her boss had broken his promise to her in order to help her to deal with this in a healthier way.

4. Help her to see the only things that she can change are her emotional and behavioural 'Cs' and her thinking 'C' (if you have identified this 'C' as well). Summarise this in another goal-oriented 'situational ABC' – which I suggest that you put next to the problem-based

'situational ABC' – under the heading 'Goal'. Thus, with Linda, I would have written the following.

Problem	Goal
Situation Going to see my boss in his office at lunchtime to talk about me not being promoted	*Situation* Going to see my boss in his office at lunchtime to talk about me not being promoted
'A' My boss broke his promise to me	'A' My boss broke his promise to me
'B' Not yet assessed	'B' Not yet assessed
'C' Emotional 'C': Problematic anger Behavioural 'C': Feeling like shouting abuse at him and giving him a slap	'C' Emotional 'C' goal: Alternative emotion (negative and healthy) Behavioural 'C' goal: Alternative overt behaviour or action tendency (constructive)

At this point you can either focus on your coachee's behavioural response to 'A' or on her emotional response to 'A'. As I focused first on Linda's behavioural response, I will start with that.

5. Have your coachee focus on her problematic behavioural response to 'A' and ask her what the consequences of her overt behaviour were (or would be) or what the impact of suppressing her action tendencies was (or would be). Once your coachee recognises the negative consequences of her overt behaviour and the negative impact of her suppressed action tendencies, ask her what behavioural response would be (1) realistic, (2) healthy and (3) acceptable to her. Stress that a realistic behavioural response is one that reflects the negativity of the 'A', a healthy response is one that is in the person's short- and

long-term interests and an acceptable response is one which the person can commit to implementing.

In Linda's case, I would have helped her to choose 'asserting myself with my boss and advancing rational arguments to encourage him to keep his promise to promote me' as her behavioural goal since she considered that it met the three criteria of realism, health and acceptability.

6. You are now in a position to help the coachee to construct an emotional goal. This emotion should also meet the criteria of realism, health and acceptability. Thus, the emotion should realistically be negative given that the 'A' to which it is a response is negative. As a rule of thumb the intensity of this emotion should reflect how negatively your coachee sees 'A'. The more negatively she views 'A', the stronger her HNE will be. The emotion should be healthy in that it should be in the person's healthy interests and accompany and facilitate her behavioural response discussed above. Finally, it should be one which the coachee can commit to experiencing and in this sense it should also have a name that is acceptable to the coachee.

Linda chose 'constructive anger' as her emotional goal in that it made sense to her, and she could see it was healthy and would help her to assert herself and express rational reasons why her boss should ideally keep his promise to promote her. It was also a realistic response to her boss breaking his promise to her and the strength of the emotion matched her negative evaluation of 'A'.

We are now in a position to present Linda's completed problem and goal 'situational ABC' below.

Problem	Goal
Situation	Situation
Going to see my boss in his office at lunchtime to talk about me not being promoted	Going to see my boss in his office at lunchtime to talk about me not being promoted

Problem	Goal
'A' My boss broke his promise to me	'A' My boss broke his promise to me
'B' Not yet assessed	'B' Not yet assessed
'C' Emotional 'C': Problematic anger	'C' Emotional 'C' goal: Constructive anger
Behavioural 'C': Feeling like shouting abuse at him and giving him a slap	Behavioural 'C' goal: Asserting myself with my boss and advancing rational reasons to encourage him to keep his promise to support me

Step 10: Help your coachee to understand the 'B'–'C' connection and identify their rigid and extreme basic attitudes and their alternative flexible and non-extreme basic attitudes and make the appropriate connections with 'C'

When working on the specific example of your coachee's emotional problem, you have identified the following:

• the situation in which it occurred
• her disturbed emotion and unconstructive behaviour (and perhaps even her highly distorted subsequent thinking), all of which occur at 'C'
• what she found most disturbing in the situation that is her adversity at 'A'
• her emotional and behavioural goals (and perhaps even her thinking goals) that represent realistic and healthy ways of responding to which she is willing to commit.

The next step is to help her to understand what we in RECBT call the 'B'–'C' connection, which is the heart of RECBT. By helping your coachee grasp this connection, you are helping her to understand that the adversity she was or will be facing at 'A' does not determine her responses at 'C'; rather it is the attitudes that she holds about the adversity that largely underpin these responses.

Three ways of making the 'B'–'C' connection

There are a number of ways of doing this. Below are three options.

Ask your coachee whether 'C' is determined by 'A' or by 'B'

In the first, you merely ask your coachee whether she thinks her UNE at 'C' is determined by the adversity at 'A' or by her attitudes at 'B'. Here is how I would have used this method with Linda.

Case study: Asking Linda whether 'C' is determined by 'A' or by 'B'

WINDY: So, Linda, we now know that you experience problematic anger towards your boss for breaking his promise towards you by not promoting you. Right?

LINDA: Right.

WINDY: But what largely determines your problematic anger, his broken promise or your attitude towards his broken promise?

LINDA: Well, I'm tempted to say his broken promise because then I can blame him, but if I am honest, I guess it's my attitude towards his broken promise.

If, in her answer, your coachee shows that she understands the 'B'–'C' connection (as Linda did), then you can proceed to the next step. If not, you can use the following method known as the 100-person technique.

The 100-person technique

When you use the 100-person technique, you ask your coachee if a hundred people of the coachee's age and gender would all experience the same UNE towards the same adversity. Hopefully the coachee will say 'no', at which point you can ask what would determine their different feelings about the same adversity. Work with your coachee until you have helped her to understand the 'B'–'C' connection. Here is how I would have used this technique with Linda.

Case study: Linda

WINDY: Let me put this another way: would a hundred people of your age and gender all feel unhealthily angry towards their boss for breaking his or her promise to them?

LINDA: I guess not, no.

WINDY: What would account for their different feelings about the same adversity?

LINDA: Well, I suppose the way they looked at it.

WINDY: That's right. We say in this approach to coaching that your emotions are largely determined by your attitudes, so the next step is for us to figure out the attitudes that underpin your feelings of problematic anger.

Windy's Review Assessment Procedure (WRAP)

This technique follows on from Windy's Magic Question (WMQ) discussed above. Its purpose is this. Once the coachee's emotional 'C' (e.g. 'problematic anger') and 'A' (e.g. 'my boss broke his promise to me') have been assessed, this technique can be used to identify both the client's rigid attitude and alternative flexible attitude and to help the client to understand the two relevant 'B'–'C' connections. This technique can also be used with any of the three extreme and non-extreme attitude pairings (i.e. awfulising attitude vs. non-awfulising attitude; discomfort intolerance attitude vs. discomfort tolerance attitude; devaluation attitude vs. unconditional acceptance attitude). I will use the case of Linda to illustrate the use of the WRAP technique.

Case study: Using the WRAP technique to help Linda identify her rigid and flexible attitudes at 'B' and see their connections with 'C'

1. Tell your coachee that you are going to review what you know and don't know so far.

WINDY: Let's review what we know and what we don't know so far. OK?
LINDA: OK.

2. Tell your client that you both know three things so far. The coachee's 'C', 'A' and what is important to them which is the part of their attitude that is common to both their rigid attitude and their flexible attitude.

WINDY: We know three things. First, we know that you experienced problematic anger ('C'). Second, we know that you were problematically angry about your boss breaking his promise to you ('A'). Third, and this is an educated guess on my part, we know that it is important to you that your boss keeps his promise to you. Am I correct?
LINDA: Correct.

*[Note that what I have done here is to identify the part of
Linda's attitude that is common to both her rigid attitude
and her alternative flexible attitude, as we will see.]*

3. Now, tell your coachee that you are going to try and
    discover what you don't know, i.e. which attitude
    underpins her anger.[1]

WINDY: Now let's review what we don't know. This
is where I need your help. We don't know which of
two attitudes your problematic anger was based on.
So, when you were problematically anger about your
boss breaking his promise to you, was your problematic anger based on Attitude 1: 'It is important to me
that my boss keeps his promise to me and therefore he
absolutely must do so' ('rigid attitude') or Attitude 2: 'It
is important to me that my boss keeps his promise to
me, but sadly and regretfully he does not have to do so'
('flexible attitude')?
LINDA: *My problematic anger was based on Attitude
number 1.*

4. If necessary, help your coachee to understand that
    their UNE was based on their rigid attitude if they are
    unsure.
5. Once your coachee is clear that their UNE was based
    on their rigid attitude, make and emphasise the rigid
    attitude–unhealthy 'C' connection.

WINDY: So, let's see if we can add this point to what we
know. Can you see that your problematic anger was
based on your rigid attitude that it is important to you
that your boss keeps his promise and therefore he absolutely must do so?
LINDA: Yes, I can see that.

6. Then ask how they would feel if they really believed their alternative flexible attitude. This is the flexible attitude–healthy 'C' connection.

WINDY: Now let's suppose instead that you had a strong conviction in Attitude 2, how would you feel about your boss not keeping his promise to you if you strongly believed that while it was important to you that he kept his promise to you, sadly and regretfully it did not follow that he must do so?

LINDA: I'd still feel angry but my anger would be constructive.

7. If necessary, help your coachee to nominate a healthy negative emotion, if not immediately volunteered, and make and emphasise the flexible attitude–healthy 'C' connection.

8. Have the client clearly understand the differences between the two 'B'–'C' connections.

WINDY: So which attitude underpins which emotion?

LINDA: Well, my problem anger is based on the rigid attitude and the constructive anger is based on the flexible attitude.

9. Help the coachee set the healthy negative emotion as the emotional goal in this situation and encourage them to see that developing conviction in their flexible attitude is the best way of achieving this goal.

WINDY: So which type of anger do you want to aim for here?

LINDA: The constructive form.

WINDY: And what are you going to have to do to achieve constructive anger?

LINDA: Practise the idea that my boss does not have to keep his promise although it is wrong of him to break his word.

Identify extreme attitudes and teach non-extreme attitudes

So far in this step, I have featured your coachee's rigid and flexible attitudes. Don't forget, however, that RECBT also holds that extreme attitudes underpin emotionally disturbed responses to adversities and that non-extreme attitudes underpin healthy responses to the same adversities.

Once you have identified your coachee's rigid attitude and related flexible attitude, you can teach her the other three extreme attitudes and the alternative non-extreme attitudes and ask her to choose the one other extreme attitude that best accounted for her UNE at 'C' (and by implication the alternative non-extreme attitude that will help her to achieve her goals). I have outlined these respective attitudes in Table 10 and illustrated them in Table 11 with Linda's attitudes being featured.

While there are three extreme attitudes, my view is that you often do not have time to identify and deal with all of them. Thus, my suggestion is that when identifying the extreme attitudes that account for the specific example of your coachee's emotional problem, help your coachee to identify the one extreme attitude that she believes accounted for her UNE in the selected example. Then help her to identify the one non-extreme attitude that is the alternative to the selected extreme attitude.

Case study: Using a shortened version of the WRAP technique to help Linda identify her devaluation and unconditional acceptance attitudes and their connections with 'C'

Let me show how I used a shortened version of the WRAP technique to identify Linda's devaluation attitude and alternative unconditional acceptance attitude and encourage her to see their connections with 'C'

> *WINDY:* OK, Linda, now as you anticipate feeling problem-
> atic anger towards your boss for breaking his promise
> to promote you, I want to see if I can understand and
> help you to understand the attitude towards your boss
> that stems from your rigid attitude and accounts for
> your problematic anger towards him. Now we know
> that you think that it is bad that your boss broke his
> promise to promote you, but when you are problematic-
> ally angry, do you believe that he is bad for acting badly
> or do you believe that he is not bad, but a fallible human
> being for acting badly?
> *LINDA:* I believe he is bad.
> *WINDY:* And how would you feel if you believed that he
> is not bad, but a fallible human being for acting badly?
> *LINDA:* Constructively angry.

Now that I have helped Linda to see the link between her rigid
attitude and extreme other-devaluation attitude and her problematic
anger, on the one hand, and the link between her flexible attitude and
non-extreme, unconditional other-acceptance attitude and her constructive anger, on the other, she is ready to make a commitment to
pursue her emotional and/or behavioural goals and to see that changing her rigid and extreme attitudes is the best way of doing this. In
the next step, I will show how you can elicit this commitment.

Step 11: Elicit commitment from the coachee to pursue her emotional and/or behavioural goals and help her to see that changing her rigid and extreme attitudes is the best way of doing this

I have stressed in this practical sequence that it is very important
for you to engage your coachee in a discussion concerning what
constitutes a healthy alternative to her emotional problem (UNE

Table 10 Rigid and extreme attitudes and flexible and non-extreme attitudes

Rigid and Extreme Attitudes	Flexible and Non-extreme Attitudes
Rigid Attitude: I want X to happen and therefore it must do so.	**Flexible Attitude**: I want X to happen, but sadly and regretfully it does not have to do so.
Awfulising Attitude: It is bad if X happens and therefore it is awful.	**Non-awfulising Attitude:** It is bad if X happens, but it is not awful.
Discomfort Intolerance Attitude: It is hard for me to tolerate it if X happens and therefore I can't tolerate it.	**Discomfort Tolerance Attitude:** It is hard for me to tolerate it if X happens, but I can tolerate it. It is worth tolerating and I am both willing to do so and going to do so.
Devaluation Attitude: It is bad if X happens and if it does, I am bad (if I am responsible), you are bad (if you are responsible) and life is bad (if life is responsible).	**Unconditional Acceptance Attitude:** It is bad if X happens and if it does, I am not bad, but fallible (if I am responsible), you are not bad, but fallible (if you are responsible), and life is not bad, but a complex mixture of good, bad and neutral aspects (if life is responsible).

and/or dysfunctional behaviour) at 'C'. However, such an appreciation has to be backed up by your coachee making a commitment to work towards this healthy emotion/functional behaviour. In this step, I will discuss how you can elicit such a commitment together with an understanding that the best way your coachee can achieve her goals is to change her rigid and extreme attitudes.

Dealing with your coachee's doubts, reservations and objections to committing herself to her emotional goals

As you do this, you may need to identify and respond to your coachee's doubts, reservations and objections to this new 'C'. Let me illustrate what I mean.

Table 11 Linda's rigid and extreme attitudes and flexible and non-extreme attitudes

Rigid and Extreme Attitudes	*Flexible and Non-extreme Attitudes*
Rigid Attitude:	**Flexible Attitude:**
I want my boss to keep his promise to me and therefore he must do so.	I want my boss to keep his promise to me, but sadly and regretfully he does not have to do so.
Awfulising Attitude:	**Non-awfulising Attitude:**
It is bad that my boss broke his promise to me and therefore it is awful.	It is bad that my boss broke his promise to me, but it is not awful.
Discomfort Intolerance Attitude:	**Discomfort Tolerance Attitude:**
It is hard for me to tolerate my boss breaking his promise to me and therefore I can't tolerate it.	It is hard for me to tolerate my boss breaking his promise to me, but I can tolerate it. It is worth tolerating and I am both willing to do so and going to do so/
Devaluation Attitude:	**Unconditional Acceptance Attitude:**
It is bad that my boss broke his promise to me and therefore he is a bad person for doing so.	It is bad that my boss broke his promise to me. But he is not a bad person for doing so. He is a fallible person who did the wrong thing.

Case study: Eliciting commitment from Linda to pursue her emotional and/or behavioural goals and helping her to see that changing her rigid and extreme attitudes is the best way of doing this

WINDY: OK, Linda, so you can see that your rigid attitude and other-devaluation attitudes underpin your problematic anger towards your boss and that your flexible attitude and unconditional other-acceptance attitudes underpin your feelings of constructive anger. So if you want to feel constructively angry instead of problematically angry towards your boss, what do you need to change?

LINDA: My rigid and extreme attitudes.

WINDY: Would you like to make a commitment to doing this or do you have some doubts or reservations about doing so?

LINDA: Well, I have one reservation.

WINDY: What's that?

LINDA: If I am constructively angry, then my feelings will be light and won't reflect the badness of what my boss did to me.

[Windy's observation: This is a common misconception about healthy negative feelings that coachees have. In reality, because flexible and non-extreme attitudes can be strongly held and reflect the importance of what your coachee wants, but does not demand, an HNE can vary in intensity according to this level of importance. Thus, constructive anger can be mild, moderate or strong depending upon how important your coachee's flexible attitude.]

WINDY: Not necessarily. For example, if your flexible and non-extreme attitude is as follows: 'I mildly want my boss to keep his promise, but he does not have to do so', then the intensity of your constructive anger will be mild or light if he breaks his promise. If your attitude is: 'I moderately want my boss to keep his promise, but he does not have to do so', then your constructive anger will be moderate if he breaks his promise. And finally, if your attitude is: 'I very strongly want my boss to keep his promise, but he still does not have to do so', then your constructive anger will be very strong when your boss breaks his promise. So, you see, your constructive anger can reflect the badness of what your boss did as long as the preference part of your flexible attitude is strong. Does that answer your reservation?

LINDA: Very much so.

Dealing with your coachee's wish to change 'A'

When you ask your coachee to commit herself to pursuing her emotional goals about 'A', she may still say that she wants to change 'A' first. If so, you need to explain to your coachee that the best time to change 'A' is when she is not disturbed about 'A' and that her disturbance about 'A' will interfere with her change attempts. Once she understands this and that the best way to be undisturbed about 'A' is by holding flexible and non-extreme attitudes towards it, she is ready to question her rigid and extreme attitudes towards 'A'. Here is how to intervene when your coachee's disturbance is largely emotional in nature.

Case study: Linda

WINDY: Is it best to change your boss's mind about not giving you the promised promotion when you are feeling problematically angry (UNE) or when you are feeling constructively anger (HNE)?

LINDA: When I feel constructively annoyed.

[Windy's observation: If Linda had said her problematic anger (i.e. her UNE), I would have endeavoured to discover the reasons for her response and then correct any misconceptions that I found.]

WINDY: And based on what we have discussed what do you need to change in order to feel constructively angry (HNE), but not problematically angry (UNE), about your boss breaking his promise to you?

LINDA: My rigid and extreme attitude.

[Windy's observation: I would have intervened if she gave any other answer, once again eliciting her reasons and then correcting any misconceptions she expressed.]

> *WINDY:* And are you committed to doing this before trying to get him to change his mind?
> *LINDA:* Yes.

Your coachee is now ready to question her rigid and extreme attitudes.

Step 12: Question both rigid and flexible attitudes together and extreme and non-extreme attitudes together

When you question your coachee's attitudes (both rigid/extreme and flexible/non-extreme), your goal is to help her see that her rigid and extreme attitudes are toxic and her flexible and non-extreme attitudes are healthy. This is known as intellectual insight because while the coachee understands this point, she does not yet have deep conviction in it to the extent that it influences, for the better, her feelings and behaviour. This 'emotional insight' will come about later in the process, when you help her to strengthen her conviction in her flexible and non-extreme attitude and weaken her conviction in her rigid and extreme attitude.

The following list shows the characteristics of both rigid/extreme and flexible/non-extreme attitudes and you should employ these characteristics in your questioning.

Rigid and extreme attitudes	Flexible and non-extreme attitudes
Rigid or extreme	Flexible or non-extreme
False	True
Illogical	Logical
Leads to unconstructive results	Leads to constructive results

For your coachee to achieve such intellectual insight, she has to question both her rigid and extreme attitudes and her flexible and non-extreme attitudes.

Please note that I suggest that you question your coachee's rigid and flexible attitudes (unless there is a good reason not to) and the one other extreme and non-extreme attitude that your coachee can see is the most appropriate one to question.

Given that time is often at a premium in coaching, I recommend that you help your coachee question their rigid vs. flexible attitude together and their selected extreme vs. non-extreme attitude together and I will outline this strategy in this book.

One final point, before I consider how to question your coachee's attitudes. As you do so, note which points she finds particularly persuasive concerning seeing that her rigid and extreme attitudes are problematic and her flexible and non-extreme attitudes are constructive. Note these arguments and capitalise on them as you proceed.

Step 13: Question a rigid attitude and a flexible attitude

Rigid attitude	Flexible attitude
I want X to happen and therefore it must do so.	I want X to happen, but sadly and regretfully it does not have to do so.

I recommend that you use three main questions when questioning your coachee's rigid attitude and flexible attitude: the empirical question, the logical question and the pragmatic question. Then, you can ask which attitude the coachee wants to strengthen and which she wants to weaken and why.

First, help your coachee to focus on her rigid attitude and her flexible attitude alternative. Have her write it down side by side (as above) or write it down yourself on a whiteboard (again as above). Then move on to the three questions. I will present them in a certain sequence. This sequence is only a guide and other sequences are fine. I will use my work with Linda to illustrate these points.

The empirical question

> WINDY: Which of the following attitudes is true and which is false and why? Your rigid attitude: 'I want my boss to keep his promise to me and therefore he must do so' or your flexible attitude: 'I want my boss to keep his promise to me, but sadly and regretfully he does not have to do so'?

According to RECBT theory, the only correct answer to this question is that the flexible attitude is true and the rigid attitude is false. Help your coachee understand the following.

- A rigid attitude is inconsistent with reality. For such an attitude to be true the demanded conditions would already have to exist when they do not. Or as soon as the coachee makes her demand, then these demanded conditions would have to come into existence. Both positions are patently inconsistent with reality.
- On the other hand, a flexible attitude is true since its two component parts are true. Your coachee can prove that she has a particular desire and can provide reasons why she wants what she wants. She can also prove that she does not have to get what she desires.

If your coachee gives you any other answer, then help her through discussion to see why her answer is incorrect and help her to accept the correct answer.

The logical question

> WINDY: Which of the following attitudes is logical and which is illogical and why? Your rigid attitude: 'I want my boss to keep his promise to me and therefore he must do so' or your flexible attitude: I want my boss

to keep his promise to me, but sadly and regretfully he does not have to do so'?

Your coachee needs to acknowledge that her rigid attitude is illogical, while her flexible attitude is logical. Help her to see that her rigid attitude is based on the same desire as her flexible attitude, but that she transforms it as follows. Here is Linda's transformation:

'I want my boss to keep his promise to me...and therefore he must do so.'

Show her that this attitude has two components. The first component which I call her 'desire' ['I want my boss to keep his promise to me...'] is not rigid, while the second component which I call her 'demand' ['...and therefore he must do so'] is rigid. As such, her rigid attitude isn't logical since one cannot logically derive something rigid from something that is not rigid. Use the template in Figure 1 with your coachee to illustrate this visually, if necessary.

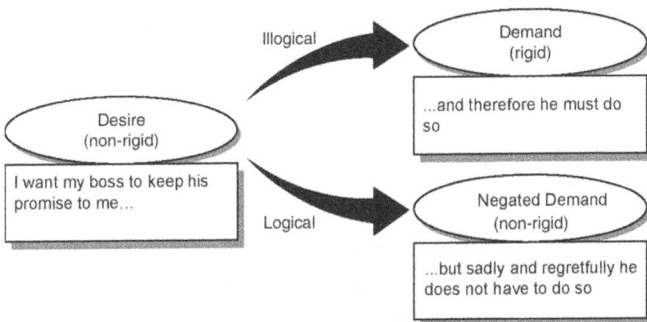

Figure 1 A rigid attitude (desire + demand) is illogical and a flexible attitude (desire + negated demand) is logical

Linda's flexible attitude is as follows:

'I want my boss to keep his promise to me, but sadly and regretfully he does not have to do so.'

Show your coachee that her flexible attitude also has two components. The first component is her 'desire' (as we have seen) ['I want my boss to keep his promise to me...'] and is not rigid, and the second component which I call her 'negated demand' ['...but sadly and regretfully he does not have to do so'] is also not rigid.

Thus, her flexible attitude is logical since both parts are not rigid and thus the second component logically follows from the first. Again, use the template in Figure 1 with your coachee to illustrate this visually, if necessary.

If your coachee gives you any other answer, then help her through discussion to see why her answer is incorrect and help her to accept the correct answer.

The pragmatic question

> WINDY: Which of the following attitudes leads to largely good results and which leads to largely poor results and why? Your rigid attitude: 'I want my boss to keep his promise to me and therefore he must do so' or your flexible attitude: 'I want my boss to keep his promise to me, but sadly and regretfully he does not have to do so'?

You need to help your coachee acknowledge that her rigid attitude leads to unhealthy results for her, while her flexible attitude leads to healthier results. As you do this, use the information provided by your coachee when you discussed the two 'B'–'C' connections (see Step 10).

If your coachee thinks that her rigid attitude leads to healthier consequences than her flexible attitude, help her through discussion to see why she is likely to be wrong.

Assess the coachee's commitment to attitude change

You can then assess your coachee's commitment to changing her attitude by asking a question such as:

> 'Which attitude do you want to strengthen and which do you want to weaken and why?'

After the questioning you have undertaken, your coachee 'should' indicate that she wishes to work to strengthen her conviction in her flexible attitude and to weaken her conviction in her rigid attitude and be able to give coherent reasons why based on her problematic feelings and behaviour and her goals for change. If your coachee gives you any other answer, then discover the reasons for this answer and work with her until she states a genuine commitment to the flexible attitude.

As part of assessing such commitment, it is worth asking your coachee whether she has any doubts, reservations and objections to strengthening her flexible attitude and weakening her rigid attitude. If she has any such doubts, respond to them with tact, and until your coachee has relinquished her reservations. See Dryden (2001) for a fuller discussion of this issue.

Case study: Questioning Linda's rigid and flexible attitudes together

WINDY: OK, Linda, let's begin questioning your attitudes, by looking at your rigid attitude and flexible attitude which I am going to write up on the whiteboard.

I then write up the following:

Rigid attitude: It's important to me that my boss not break his promise to promote me...and therefore he absolutely should not have done so.

Flexible attitude: It's important to me that my boss not break his promise to promote me...but sadly and regretfully he does not have to do what I want him to do.

WINDY: Now if you look at these two attitudes, which is true and which is false?

LINDA: My rigid attitude is false and my flexible attitude is true.

WINDY: Why is that?

LINDA: Well, it's true that I want my boss not to break his promise, but it's not true that he must do what I want him to do.

WINDY: Why not?

LINDA: Because he is in charge of his decisions and I am not.

WINDY: Is that a persuasive argument for you?

[*Windy's observation: In my view it is important that a coachee develops persuasive arguments in favour of her flexible and non-extreme attitudes and against her rigid and extreme attitudes.*]

LINDA: Well, yes, I was brought up to think that people in authority were honourable and kept their promises. I now see that this is true for some people, but not all. And my boss does not have to be the way I want him to be in this respect. He is the way he is. So that is a good argument.

WINDY: OK. Now which of these two attitudes is sensible and which is not?

LINDA: Again, my flexible attitude is sensible and my rigid attitude is not.

WINDY: Why?

LINDA: Because there is no logical connection between what I want and what has to be.

WINDY: Is that persuasive?

LINDA: Kind of, but not as persuasive as the idea that my boss does not have to be the way I want him to be. He is the way he is.

WINDY: OK, now which of these attitudes is healthier for you and which is less healthy?

LINDA: My flexible attitude is better for me in all sorts of ways.

WINDY: Can you name a few?

LINDA: Well, it will help me to be relatively calm when I talk to him. It will help me to adjust constructively if I can't get him to change his mind and promote me, and it will help me to concentrate on other things.

WINDY: Whereas your rigid attitude?

LINDA: Well, it gives me the results I have already discussed with you. I feel like exploding with him, which isn't good if I am going to have a meeting with him. It leads to rumination and I can't concentrate on my coaching work with you.

WINDY: Is that a persuasive argument?

LINDA: Very!

WINDY: So I suggest that you make a note of those two persuasive arguments.

LINDA: OK.

WINDY: Finally, which of these two attitudes do you want to commit to strengthening?

LINDA: My flexible attitude.

WINDY: Do you have any reservations about giving up your demand?

[*Windy's observation: Sometimes coachees have doubts, reservations and objections to changing their rigid and extreme*

> *attitudes. It is best to know about them so you can respond to them. If your coachee harbours any such doubts, for example, and you don't know about them, they will interfere with your coachee changing her rigid and extreme attitudes.*]

LINDA: Well, when I think that he must keep his promise, I hold on to a view of the world where fairness triumphs in the end and it's tough giving that up.

WINDY: Do you think that holding that attitude makes fairness triumph in the end?

LINDA: Sadly, no.

WINDY: Does acknowledging that help?

LINDA: Well, it's like swallowing a bitter pill. It will do you good, but it doesn't taste nice.

WINDY: So is it worth it to swallow the bitter pill and commit yourself to your flexible attitude?

LINDA: Yes, it is.

Step 14: Question an awfulising attitude and a non-awfulising attitude

Awfulising attitude	Non-awfulising attitude
It would be bad if X happens and therefore it would be terrible.	It would be bad but not terrible if X happens.

When questioning your coachee's awfulising and non-awfulising attitudes, use the same three questions that you used to question her rigid and flexible attitudes: i.e. the empirical question, the logical question and the pragmatic question. Once you have done this, you can then ask which attitude the coachee wants to strengthen and which she wants to weaken and why.

First, help your coachee to focus on her awfulising attitude and her non-awfulising attitude alternative. Again ask her to write it down side by side (as above) or write it down yourself on a white-board (again as above). Then move on to the three questions.

The empirical question

> WINDY: Which of the following attitudes is true and which is false and why? Awfulising attitude (iB): It is bad and therefore terrible that my boss broke his promise to me. Non-awfulising attitude (rB): It is bad that my boss broke his promise to me, but it is not terrible.

According to RECBT theory, an awfulising attitude is false and a non-awfulising attitude is true.

When questioning your coachee's awfulising attitude, help your coachee to see that when she is holding this attitude, she believes the following:

- Nothing could be worse.
- The event in question is worse than 100% bad.
- No good could possibly come from this bad event.
- The event cannot possibly be transcended or surmounted.

Help her to see that all four convictions are inconsistent with reality and that her non-awfulising attitude is true since this is made up of the following ideas:

- Things could always be worse.
- The event in question is less than 100% bad.
- Good could come from this bad event.
- The event can be transcended or surmounted.

If your coachee gives you answers that are at variance with the above, then help her through discussion to see why her answers are incorrect and help her to accept the correct answer.

The logical question

> *WINDY:* Which of the following attitudes is logical and
> which is illogical and why? Awfulising attitude: It is bad
> and therefore terrible that my boss broke his promise
> to me. Non-awfulising attitude: It is bad that my boss
> broke his promise to me, but it is not terrible.

Help your coachee see that her awfulising attitude is illogical,
while her non-awfulising attitude is logical. Show her that her
awfulising attitude is based on the same evaluation of badness as
her non-awfulising attitude, but she transforms this as follows:

> 'It is bad that my boss broke his promise to promote me…and
> therefore it is terrible.'

Show her that her awfulising attitude has two components. The
first component which I call 'evaluation of badness' ['It is bad that
my boss broke his promise to me…'] is non-extreme, while the
second component which I call 'awfulising' ['…and therefore it is
terrible'] is extreme. As such, help her to see that her awfulising
attitude is illogical since one cannot logically derive something
extreme from something that is not extreme. Use the template in
Figure 2 with your coachee to illustrate this visually, if necessary.
    Your coachee's non-awfulising attitude is as follows:

> 'It is bad that my boss broke his promise to me…but it is not
> terrible.'

Encourage your coachee to see that her non-awfulising attitude
also has two components. The first is 'evaluation of badness' (as
shown above) ['It is bad that my boss broke his promise to me…']
and is non-extreme and the second component which I call 'non-
awfulising' is also non-extreme ['…but it is not terrible']. Thus,
help her to see that her non-awfulising attitude is logical since

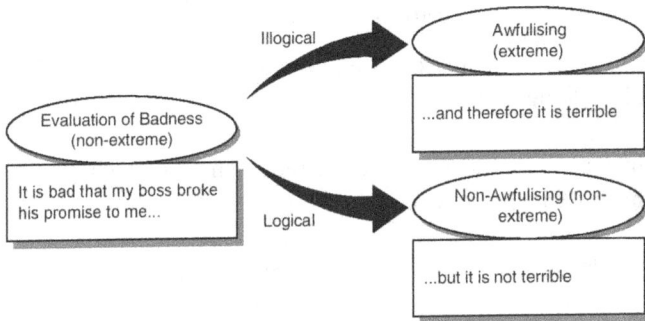

Figure 2 An awfulising attitude (evaluation of badness + awfulising) is illogical and a non-awfulising attitude (evaluation of badness + non-awfulising) is logical

both parts of it are non-extreme and thus the second component logically follows from the first. Again, use the template in Figure 2 with your coachee to illustrate this visually, if necessary.

The pragmatic question

> WINDY: Which of the following attitudes leads to largely good results and which leads to largely poor results and why? Awfulising attitude: It is bad and therefore terrible that my boss broke his promise to me. Non-awfulising attitude: It is bad that my boss broke his promise to me, but it is not terrible.

You need to help your coachee acknowledge that her awfulising attitude leads to unhealthy results for her, while her non-awfulising attitude leads to healthier results. As you do this, again use the information provided by your coachee when you discussed the two 'B'–'C' connections (see Step 10).

If your coachee thinks that her awfulising attitude leads to healthier consequences than her non-awfulising attitude, help her through discussion to see why she is likely to be wrong.

Assess the coachee's commitment to attitude change

You can then assess your coachee's commitment to changing her attitude by asking a question such as:

> 'Which attitude do you want to strengthen and which do you want to weaken and why?'

After the questioning you have undertaken, your coachee 'should' indicate that she wishes to work to strengthen her conviction in her non-awfulising attitude and to weaken her conviction in her awfulising attitude and be able to give coherent reasons for her answer. If your coachee gives you any other answer, then discover the reasons for this answer and work with her until she states a genuine commitment to her non-awfulising attitude.

Again, as part of assessing such commitment, it is worth asking your coachee whether she has any doubts, reservations and objections to strengthening her non-awfulising attitude and weakening her awfulising attitude. If she has any such doubts, respond to them with tact, and until your coachee has relinquished her reservations (see Dryden, 2001).

Step 15: Question a discomfort intolerance attitude and a discomfort tolerance attitude

Discomfort intolerance attitude	Discomfort tolerance attitude
It is hard for me to tolerate it if X happens and therefore I can't tolerate it.	It is hard for me to tolerate it if X happens, but I can tolerate it. It is worth tolerating and I am both willing to do so and going to do so.

When questioning your coachee's discomfort intolerance attitude and discomfort tolerance attitude, again use the tripartite questioning approach: the empirical question, the logical question and the pragmatic question. Once you have done this again, ask which attitude the coachee wants to strengthen and which she wants to weaken and why.

Once again begin by suggesting that your coachee focus on her discomfort intolerance attitude and her discomfort tolerance alternative. Again, ask her to write it down side by side (as above) or write it down yourself on a whiteboard (again as above). Then move on to the three questions.

The empirical question

> WINDY: Which of the following attitudes is true and which is false and why? Discomfort intolerance attitude: It is hard for me to tolerate my boss breaking his promise to me and therefore I can't tolerate it. Discomfort tolerance attitude: It is hard for me to tolerate my boss breaking his promise to me, but I can tolerate it. It is worth tolerating and I am both willing to do so and going to do so.

According to RECBT theory, a discomfort tolerance attitude is true and a discomfort intolerance attitude is false.

When questioning your coachee's discomfort intolerance attitude, help your coachee to see that when she is holding this attitude, she believes *at the time* the following:

- I will die or disintegrate if the discomfort continues to exist.
- I will lose the capacity to experience happiness if the discomfort continues to exist.

Help her to see that both these convictions are inconsistent with reality and that her discomfort tolerance attitude is true since this is made up of the following ideas:

- I will struggle if the discomfort continues to exist, but I will neither die nor disintegrate.

- I will not lose the capacity to experience happiness if the discomfort continues to exist, although this capacity will be temporarily diminished.
- The discomfort is worth tolerating.
- I am both willing to tolerate it and am going to do so.

If your coachee gives you answers that are at variance with the above, then help her through discussion to see why her answers are incorrect and help her to accept the correct answer.

The logical question

> WINDY: Which of the following attitudes is logical and which is illogical and why? Discomfort intolerance attitude: It is hard for me to tolerate my boss breaking his promise to me and therefore I can't tolerate it. Discomfort tolerance attitude: It is hard for me to tolerate my boss breaking his promise to me, but I can tolerate it. It is worth tolerating and I am both willing to do so and going to do so.

Help your coachee to see that her discomfort intolerance attitude is illogical, while her discomfort tolerance attitude is logical.

Show her that her discomfort intolerance attitude is based on the same idea of struggle as her discomfort tolerance attitude, but she transforms this as follows:

> 'It is hard for me to bear it that my boss broke his promise to me…and therefore I can't bear it.'

Show your coachee that her discomfort intolerance attitude has two components. The first component which is what I call 'struggle' ['It is hard for me to bear it that my boss broke his promise to promote me…'] is non-extreme, while the second component which I call 'discomfort intolerance' ['...and therefore I can't bear it'] is extreme. As such help her to see that her discomfort intolerance attitude is illogical since one cannot logically derive something extreme from something that is not extreme. Use the template in Figure 3 with your coachee to illustrate this visually, if necessary.

Your coachee's discomfort tolerance attitude is as follows:

> 'It is hard for me to bear it that my boss broke his promise to promote me...but I can bear it. It is worth tolerating and I am both willing to do so and going to do so.'

Encourage your coachee to see that her discomfort tolerance attitude has five components. The first is 'struggle' (as shown above) ['It is hard for me to bear it that my boss broke his promise to me...'] and is non-extreme and the following four components which I call 'discomfort tolerance' are all non-extreme ['...but I can bear it. It is worth tolerating and I am both willing to do so and going to do so']. Thus, help her to see that her discomfort tolerance attitude is logical since all parts of it are non-extreme and thus the last four components logically follow from the first. Again, use the template in Figure 3 with your coachee to illustrate this visually, if necessary.

The pragmatic question

WINDY: Which of the following attitudes leads to largely good results and which leads to largely poor results and why? Discomfort tolerance attitude: It is hard for me to tolerate my boss breaking his promise to me and therefore I can't tolerate it. Discomfort tolerance attitude: It is hard for me to tolerate my boss breaking his promise to me, but I can tolerate it. It is worth tolerating and I am both willing to do so and going to do so.

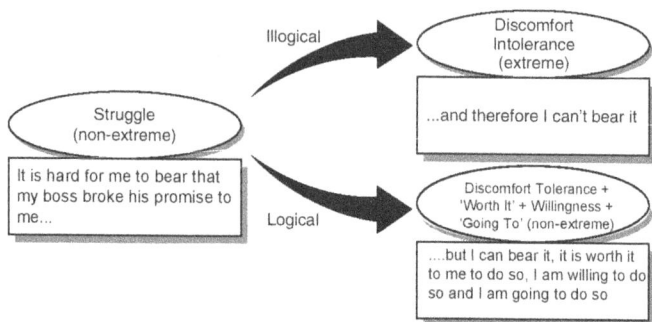

Figure 3 A discomfort intolerance attitude (struggle + discomfort intolerance) is illogical and a discomfort tolerance attitude (struggle + discomfort tolerance + 'worth it' + 'willingness' + 'going to') is logical

You need to help your coachee acknowledge that her discomfort intolerance attitude leads to unhealthy results for her, while her discomfort tolerance attitude leads to healthier results. As you do this, once again use the information provided by your coachee when you discussed the two 'B'–'C' connections if you need to (see Step 10).

Assess the coachee's commitment to attitude change

You can then assess your coachee's commitment to changing her attitude by asking a question such as:

'Which attitude do you want to strengthen and which do you want to weaken and why?'

After the questioning you have undertaken, your coachee 'should' indicate that she wishes to work to strengthen her conviction in her discomfort tolerance attitude and to weaken her conviction in her discomfort intolerance attitude and be able to give coherent reasons for her answer. If your coachee gives you any other answer, then discover the reasons for this answer and work with her until she states a genuine commitment to her discomfort tolerance attitude.

As part of assessing such commitment, it is worth asking your coachee once again whether she has any doubts, reservations and objections to strengthening her discomfort tolerance attitude and weakening her discomfort intolerance attitude. If she has any such doubts, respond to them with tact, and until your coachee has relinquished her reservations (see Dryden, 2001, for a fuller discussion of this issue).

Step 16: Question a devaluation attitude and an unconditional acceptance attitude

Devaluation attitude	Unconditional acceptance attitude
It is bad if X happens and if it does, I am bad (if I am responsible), you are bad (if you are responsible) and life is bad (if life is responsible).	It is bad if X happens and if it does, I am not bad, but fallible (if I am responsible), you are not bad, but fallible (if you are responsible), and life is not bad, but a complex mixture of good, bad and neutral aspects (if life is responsible).

When questioning your coachee's devaluation and acceptance attitudes, once again use the following three questions: the empirical question, the logical question and the pragmatic question. As before, once you have done this, ask which attitude the coachee wants to strengthen and which she wants to weaken and why.

Again suggest that your coachee focus on her devaluation attitude and her acceptance attitude alternative. Ask her to write it down side by side (as above) or write it down yourself on a whiteboard (again as above). Then move on to the three questions.

The empirical question

> WINDY: Which of the following attitudes is true and which is false and why? Other-devaluation attitude: It is bad that my boss broke his promise to me and therefore he is a bad person for doing so. Unconditional other-acceptance attitude: It is bad that my boss broke his promise to me. But he is not a bad person for doing so. He is a fallible person who did the wrong thing.

According to RECBT theory, an unconditional acceptance attitude is true and a devaluation attitude is false.

Questioning your coachee's person-devaluation (self- or other-) attitude

Help your coachee to see that when she is holding a person-devaluation attitude (self- or other-), she believes *at the time* the following:

- A person (self or other) can legitimately be given a single global rating that defines their essence, and the worth of a person is dependent upon conditions that change (e.g. my worth goes up when I do well and goes down when I don't do well).
- A person can be rated on the basis of one of his or her aspects.

Help her to see that these convictions are inconsistent with reality and that her unconditional person-acceptance (self- or other-) attitude is true since this is made up of the following ideas:

- A person cannot legitimately be given a single global rating that defines their essence, and their worth, as far as they have it, is not dependent upon conditions that change (e.g. my worth stays the same whether or not I do well).
- It makes sense to rate discrete aspects of a person, but it does not make sense to rate a person on the basis of these discrete aspects.

Questioning your coachee's life-devaluation attitude

Help her to see that when she is holding a life-devaluation attitude, she believes *at the time* the following:

- The world can legitimately be given a single rating that defines its essential nature, and the value of the world varies according to what happens within it (e.g. the value of the world goes up when something fair occurs and goes down when something unfair happens).
- The world can be rated on the basis of one of its aspects.

Help her to see that these convictions are inconsistent with reality and that her unconditional life-acceptance attitude is true since this is made up of the following ideas:

- The world cannot legitimately be given a single rating that defines its essential nature, and the value of the world does not vary according to what happens within it (e.g. the value of the world stays the same whether fairness exists at any given time or not).
- It makes sense to rate discrete aspects of the world, but it does not make sense to rate the world on the basis of these discrete aspects.

If your coachee gives you answers that are at variance with the above, then help her through discussion to see why her answers are incorrect and help her to accept the correct answer.

The logical question

WINDY: Which of the following attitudes is logical and which is illogical and why? Other-devaluation attitude: It is bad that my boss broke his promise to me and therefore he is a bad person for doing so. Unconditional other-acceptance attitude: It is bad that my boss broke his promise to me. But he is not a bad person for doing so. He is a fallible person who did the wrong thing.

Help your coachee see that her devaluation attitude is illogical, while her unconditional acceptance attitude is logical.

For example, you will see that Linda held an other-devaluation attitude. So, I showed her that this attitude was based on the same idea as her other-acceptance attitude in that in both she acknowledged that it was bad that her boss broke his promise to promote her, but that in her other-devaluation attitude she transformed it as follows:

'It is bad that my boss broke his promise to me...and therefore he is bad for doing so.'

Thus, her other-devaluation attitude has two components. The first ['It is bad that my boss broke his promise to promote me...'] is an evaluation of a part of her experience, while the second ['...and therefore he is bad for doing so'] is an evaluation of the whole of her boss's 'self'. As such, she is making the illogical part–whole error where the part is deemed illogically to define the whole.

Her other-acceptance attitude is as follows:

'It is bad that my boss broke his promise to me...but he is not bad for doing so. He is a fallible person who did the wrong thing.'

I encouraged Linda to see that her unconditional other-acceptance attitude is logical because it shows that the self of the other is complex and incorporates a bad event. Thus, in holding her unconditional other-acceptance attitude, she avoids making the part–whole error.

In helping your coachees to question the logic of their devaluation and acceptance attitudes, remember the part–whole error and how it can be avoided.

The pragmatic question

> WINDY: Which of the following attitudes leads to largely good results and which leads to largely poor results and why? Other-devaluation attitude: It is bad that my boss broke his promise to me and therefore he is a bad person for doing so. Unconditional other-acceptance attitude: It is bad that my boss broke his promise to me. But he is not a bad person for doing so. He is a fallible person who did the wrong thing.

You need to help your coachee acknowledge that her devaluation attitude leads to unhealthy results for her, while her unconditional acceptance attitude leads to healthier results. As before, as you do this, use the information provided by your coachee when you discussed the two 'B'–'C' connections if you need to (see Step 10).

Assess the coachee's commitment to attitude change

You can then assess your coachee's commitment to changing her attitude by again asking a question such as:

> 'Which attitude do you want to strengthen and which do you want to weaken and why?'

After the questioning you have undertaken, your coachee 'should' indicate that she wishes to work to strengthen her conviction in her acceptance attitude and to weaken her conviction in her devaluation attitude and be able to give coherent reasons for her answer. If your coachee gives you any other answer, then discover the reasons for this answer and work with her until she states a genuine commitment to her unconditional acceptance attitude.

As part of assessing such commitment, it is worth asking your coachee once again whether she has any doubts, reservations and objections to strengthening her acceptance attitude and weakening her devaluation attitude. If she has any such doubts, respond to them with tact, and until your coachee has relinquished her reservations (see Dryden, 2001, for a fuller discussion of this issue).

Case study: Questioning Linda's devaluation and unconditional acceptance attitudes together

WINDY: OK, Linda, let's continue by questioning your other-devaluation and unconditional other-acceptance attitudes, which again I am going to write up on the whiteboard.

I then write up the following:

Other-devaluation attitude: It is bad that my boss broke his promise to me and therefore he is bad for doing so.

Unconditional other-acceptance attitude: It is bad that my boss broke his promise to me, but he is not bad for doing so. He is a fallible human being who did the wrong thing.

WINDY: Now which of these two attitudes is true and which is false?

LINDA: Well, when I'm really angry, the other-devaluation attitude feels true, but I know it's not.

WINDY: Why not?

LINDA: Well, doing the wrong thing does not make my boss a bad person.

WINDY: Why not?

LINDA: Because he is ordinary and fallible. If he was bad, he would be incapable of doing good and I know that's not true.

WINDY: How do you know that?

LINDA: Because he has done good things for me before and for others too. I know his family love him and he is always showing concern for his aged mum. So there is a lot of good about him.

WINDY: As well as bad?

LINDA: As well as bad.

WINDY: Do you find any of these arguments persuasive?

LINDA: The idea that he is a complicated mixture of good and bad, rather than all bad, is particularly persuasive.

WINDY: OK, now, as you look at the two attitudes on the board, which is sensible and which is not?

LINDA: The unconditional other-acceptance is sensible and the other one isn't.

WINDY: Why is that?

LINDA: Because when I hold the other-devaluation attitude, I think that his bad behaviour towards me when he broke his promise defines him as a person, whereas when I hold the other one, I don't think that.

WINDY: Is that a persuasive argument?

LINDA: Yes it is.

WINDY: Now when you look at the two attitudes again, which is healthy for you and which isn't?

LINDA: For the same reasons as with my rigid and flexible attitudes, my other-devaluation attitude is unhealthy as it leads to explosive anger feelings, rumination and I can't get on with anything. I feel my life is on hold. My unconditional other-acceptance attitude, on the other hand, leads me to feel annoyed, but in a constructive way so that I can talk to my boss. Also, it helps me to think about other things and get on with my life.

WINDY: And which of these two attitudes do you want to commit to strengthening?

LINDA: My unconditional other-acceptance attitude.

WINDY: Do you have any reservations about giving up the other-devaluation attitude?

LINDA: Well, that attitude makes me feel powerful at the time, but that's a momentary thing. So no, not really.

Step 17: Help the coachee to strengthen her conviction in her flexible and non-extreme attitudes and weaken her conviction in her rigid and extreme attitudes

I mentioned earlier in the book (see p. 114) that there are two types of insight in RECBT: intellectual insight and emotional insight.

When your coachee has intellectual insight, she understands why her rigid and extreme attitudes are false, illogical and unhelpful and why her flexible and non-extreme attitudes are true, logical and helpful, but this insight has little impact on her feelings and behaviour. However, when your coachee has emotional insight, this understanding has great impact on her feelings and behaviour. In common parlance, when your coachee has intellectual insight into her flexible and non-extreme attitudes, she can 'talk the talk', but when she has emotional insight into these attitudes, she can 'walk the talk'.

It is useful to explain to your coachee about these different forms of insight and what she needs to do to move from intellectual insight to emotional insight.

Explain the process of change

Here is an example of how to explain the process of change.

Case study: Explaining the process of change to Linda

WINDY: So now you can see that while you would have preferred your boss not to have broken his promise to you, sadly he does not have to do what you want, and he is not bad for breaking his promise, but a fallible human being who did the wrong thing. But how much do you believe that right now?

LINDA: Well, I can understand it, but I don't believe it.

WINDY: What do you need to do to believe it?

LINDA: I guess I need to practise the new attitude and to act on it.

[Windy's observation: Linda has articulated the two main ingredients for change: practice and action.]

WINDY: Exactly, but bearing in mind that you have stronger conviction in your rigid and extreme attitudes than your flexible and non-extreme attitudes even though you can see that they are false, illogical and unhelpful, how comfortable will you be when you do practise and act on your flexible and non-extreme attitudes?

LINDA: I guess not that comfortable.

WINDY: That's right. And what would you need to do to be more comfortable with your flexible and non-extreme attitudes?

LINDA: Keep practising them?

WINDY: That's right. Keep practising them and acting on them while tolerating the discomfort, and as you do so your conviction in them will grow.

A selection of techniques to help your coachee gain conviction in her flexible and non-extreme attitudes

There are a number of techniques that you can use to help your coachee to practise and act on her flexible and non-extreme attitudes. I will review a few here and suggest that you consult Dryden (2001) if you are interested in learning more about such techniques.

Use the attack–response technique

This technique, which is sometimes called the zig-zag technique, is based on the idea that your coachee can strengthen her conviction in a flexible and non-extreme attitude by responding persuasively to attacks on this attitude. I will outline the main (written) version of the attack–response technique, but there are several other variations on the same theme described more fully in Dryden (2001).

Instructions on how to teach your coachee to complete a written attack–response form

1. Ask your coachee to write down her specific flexible and non-extreme attitude on a piece of paper.
2. Ask her to rate her present level of conviction in this attitude on a 100% point scale, with 0% = no conviction and 100% = total conviction (i.e. your coachee really believes this in her gut and it markedly influences her feelings and behaviour). Ask her to write down this rating under her attitude.
3. Ask your coachee to write down an attack on this flexible and non-extreme attitude. Her attack may take the form of a doubt, reservation or objection to this flexible and non-extreme attitude. It should also contain an explicit rigid and extreme attitude (e.g. a rigid attitude, awfulising attitude, discomfort intolerance attitude or devaluation attitude). Suggest that she make this attack as genuinely as she can. The more it reflects what she believes, the better.
4. Then tell your coachee to respond to this attack as fully as she can. It is really important that she responds to each element of the attack. In particular, make sure that she responds to rigid and extreme attitude statements and also to distorted or unrealistic inferences framed in the form of a doubt, reservation or objection to the flexible and non-extreme attitude. Encourage her to do so as persuasively as possible and to write down her response.
5. Tell your coachee to continue in this vein until she has answered all of her attacks and cannot think of any more.

Make sure throughout this process that she keeps the focus on the flexible and non-extreme attitude that she is trying to strengthen.

If your coachee finds this exercise difficult, suggest that she makes it easier by making her attacks gently at first. Then, when she finds that she can respond to these attacks quite easily, suggest that she begins to make the attacks more biting. Ask her to work in this way until she is making really strong attacks. Suggest that when she makes an attack, she does so as if she really wants to believe it. And when she responds, urge her to really throw herself into it with the intention of demolishing the attack and of strengthening her conviction in her flexible and non-extreme attitude.

Remind your coachee that the purpose of this exercise is to strengthen her conviction in her flexible and non-extreme attitude, so it is important that she stops only when she has answered all of her attacks. If she makes an attack that she cannot respond to, suggest that she stop the exercise and raise the matter with you in her next session.

6. When your coachee has answered all of her attacks, ask her to re-rate her level of conviction in her flexible and non-extreme attitude using the 0%-100% scale as before. If your coachee has succeeded at responding persuasively to her attacks, then this rating will have gone up appreciably. If it has not increased or it has only done so a little, discuss this with her so that you can both discover what is preventing an increase in flexible and non-extreme attitude conviction.

Use rational-emotive imagery

Rational-emotive imagery (REI) is an imagery method designed to help your coachee to practise changing her *specific* rigid and extreme attitude to its flexible and non-extreme equivalent while simultaneously imagining what she is most disturbed about in the specific situation in question. Help your coachee to understand that this method will help her to strengthen her conviction in her new flexible and non-extreme attitudes.

What follows is a set of instructions for using Albert Ellis's version of REI (Ellis & Maultsby, 1974).

Instructions for using REI: Ellis version

1. Ask your coachee to take a situation in which she disturbed herself and then ask her to identify the aspect of the situation she was most disturbed about.
2. Ask your coachee to close her eyes and imagine the situation as vividly as possible and to focus on the adversity at 'A'.
3. Encourage your coachee to allow herself to experience fully the UNE that she felt at the time, while still focusing intently on the 'A'. Ensure that your coachee's UNE is *one* of the following: anxiety, depression, shame, guilt, hurt, problematic anger, problematic jealousy, problematic envy.
4. Ask your coachee to really experience this disturbed emotion for a moment or two and then ask her to change her emotional response to an HNE, while all the time focusing intently on the adversity at 'A'. Ask her not to change the intensity of the emotion, just the emotion itself. Thus, if her original UNE was anxiety, encourage her to change this to concern; if it was depression, have her change it to sadness. Ask her to change shame to disappointment, guilt to remorse, hurt to sorrow, problematic anger to constructive anger, problematic jealousy to constructive jealousy and problematic envy to constructive envy. Suggest that she keep experiencing this new emotion for about five minutes, all the time focusing on the adversity at 'A'. If she goes back to the old UNE, ask her to bring the new HNE back.
5. At the end of five minutes, ask your coachee how she changed her emotion.

6. Make sure that your coachee changed her emotional response by changing her specific rigid and extreme attitude to its healthy alternative. If she did not do so (if, for example, she changed her emotion by changing the 'A' to make it less negative or neutral, or by holding an indifference attitude towards the 'A'), suggest that she does the exercise again and keep doing this until she has changed her emotion only by changing her specific unhealthy attitude to its healthy alternative.

Encourage your coachee to practise REI several times a day and encourage her to aim for 30 minutes' daily practice when she is not doing any other therapy homework.

Suggest that your coachee rehearse her flexible and non-extreme attitudes while acting in ways that are consistent with these attitudes

Perhaps the most powerful way of helping your coachee to strengthen her target flexible and non-extreme attitude is to encourage her to rehearse it while facing the relevant adversity at 'A' and while acting in ways that are consistent with this flexible and non-extreme attitude.

Thus, end a coaching session by negotiating a homework assignment that helps her to implement the above principle and is based on the work that you have already done in the session.

If you need to, help your coachee to see that when her behaviour and thinking are in sync and she keeps them in sync, she maximises the chances of strengthening her conviction in her flexible and non-extreme attitude. Conversely, discourage her from acting and thinking in ways that are consistent with her old rigid and extreme attitude.

Remember the following equation when negotiating a behavioural homework task with your coachee:

Face adversity at 'A' + Rehearse flexible and non-extreme attitude at 'B' + Act in ways consistent with this attitude at 'C'

Case study: Helping Linda to strengthen her conviction in her flexible and non-extreme attitudes and weaken her conviction in her rigid and extreme attitudes

Teaching Linda the attack–response technique

In helping Linda strengthen her conviction in her flexible and non-extreme attitudes, I first taught her the attack–response technique (see pp. 139–141) and suggested that she did it for homework. I will discuss what she did and how I responded in the section on reviewing homework.

Teaching Linda rational-emotive imagery

I then taught Linda rational-emotive imagery (see pp. 141–143). I asked her to close her eyes and imagine that when she goes into her meeting with her boss, she focuses on him breaking his promise to her. I then encouraged her to make herself problematically angry about this, which she found quite easy to do as you might imagine. Then, while still focusing on the broken promise, I asked her to make herself constructively angry about this rather than problematically angry. When she did this, I asked how she effected the change and after a few times when she gave me a benign interpretation of his behaviour (e.g. 'It wasn't his fault, it was his superiors'), she effected the change by changing her attitude to: 'He was wrong to break his promise to me, but he does not have to do the right thing. He is fallible, not bad for doing the wrong thing.' Once she understood how to change her feelings by changing her attitude, I suggested that she practise this several times a day.

Linda rehearses her flexible and non-extreme attitudes while acting in ways that are consistent with these attitudes

Perhaps the most powerful way that Linda could strengthen her conviction in her flexible and non-extreme attitude was to act in ways that are consistent with this attitude. The main way in which Linda did this was to talk to her boss about feelings of constructive anger about him breaking his promise to her. Before she did this, she rehearsed her flexible and non-extreme attitude that she put into her words (i.e. 'My boss is not bad for breaking his promise to me. He is fallible and does not have to keep his promise.') and she kept this in mind while she talked to him. I will discuss what happened in Step 19 below.

Step 18: Negotiate homework assignments

As a coach, you will be very familiar with the idea that your coachees need to put into practice what they learn in coaching sessions if they are to realise their personal development objectives. The same principle applies when you are helping a coachee to deal with her emotional problem so that she can resume working on her coaching goals. In RECBT the tasks that your coachee executes in the service of dealing effectively with her emotional problem are known as homework assignments. While they are traditionally negotiated at the end of coaching sessions, they can be agreed earlier. In which case, it is important to ensure that, at the end of the session, the coachee understands what she is going to do.

Principles in negotiating a homework assignment with your coachee

There are a number of important principles that it is important that you follow in negotiating a homework assignment with your coachee. I will briefly review them here.

Use a term for homework assignments that is acceptable to your coachee

While the generic term for a task that your coachee carries out between sessions is a homework assignment, some coachees respond negatively to the term since it reminds them of school with its negative connotations. In such cases use a term that is more acceptable to your coachee.

Negotiate an assignment with your coachee; do not assign it unilaterally

Coaching is an activity that is based on a collaborative relationship between coach and coachee. This is reflected in your stance towards homework assignments. It is important that you negotiate a homework assignment with your coachee, not assign one unilaterally.

Allow sufficient time in the session to negotiate the homework assignment properly

As you know, time is at a premium in a coaching session and you will see from the previously discussed steps that you have much to do when helping your coachee address her emotional problem effectively. So, it is easy to get to the end of the session and realise that you have not negotiated a relevant homework assignment with your coachee. The best way to avoid this is to prioritise negotiating homework assignments in your mind and even have a visible prompt that you can consult in the session as a reminder. Allocating the last ten minutes to such negotiation is a good rule of thumb.

Ensure that the homework assignment follows logically from the work you did with your coachee in the session

It is important that the assignment is relevant to the work that you have done in the session with your coachee and provides a good logical bridge between what you have discussed in the session and what your coachee has agreed to do between sessions.

Ensure that your coachee clearly understands the homework assignment

If the coachee does not understand what she has agreed to do, she is unlikely to do it.

Ensure that the homework assignment is relevant to your coachee dealing effectively with her emotional problem

If your coachee does not understand how the task she has agreed to do will help her to achieve her emotional goals and thus deal effectively with her emotional problem, she will be far less likely to do the task than if she has such understanding.

Ensure that the type of homework assignment you negotiated with your coachee is relevant to the stage reached by the two of you on her emotional problem

There are a number of different types of homework assignments and it is important that the type of assignment your coachee agrees to do is relevant to where you have got to in dealing with her emotional problem. Thus, a reading assignment is best suited to helping your coachee understand more about her emotional problem, a cognitive assignment best for giving her practice at questioning her attitudes and a cognitive-behavioural assignment best for helping her to act on her flexible and non-extreme attitude while simultaneously rehearsing it.

Employ the 'challenging but not overwhelming' principle in negotiating the homework assignment

If you ask your coachee to do something that is too much for her, then she will not do it. If you ask her to do something that is too easy for her, then there is little therapeutic value to be gained for her. However, if you suggest that she does something that she can do but will be difficult for her, then she is likely both to do it and to gain from doing so.

Introduce and explain the 'no lose' concept of homework assignments

The 'no lose' concept in homework points to the fact that when your coachee does a homework assignment successfully, then she gains from doing so. However, if she fails to do it, then this provides an opportunity to learn more about obstacles to change so that you can both effectively address such obstacles. The latter point should be particularly stressed when your coachee feels discouraged when she fails to do an assignment.

Ensure that your coachee has the necessary skills to carry out the homework assignment

If your coachee does not have the required skills to do her homework, then it is unlikely that she will do it or she will do it poorly. Thus, if Linda lacks the necessary assertive skills, then she is unlikely to speak to her boss about his broken promise to her or she will do so poorly. Therefore, if your coachee lacks the necessary skills that a particular homework assignment calls for, teach her these skills before suggesting that she implements the assignment.

Ensure that your coachee thinks that she can do the homework assignment

Your coachee may have the required skills to do the assignment, but may think that she cannot do it. Encourage her to use imagery rehearsal in the session where she pictures herself successfully completing the assignment and to practise this technique between sessions before doing the task in actuality. Such imagery rehearsal is useful in helping your coachee see that she can do what she previously thought she could not do.

Elicit a firm commitment from your coachee that she will carry out the homework assignment

It is sometimes useful to ask your coachee to make a commitment to do a homework assignment. This may be with herself, with you or with a friend. If doing so increases the chances that your coachee will carry out the assignment, then it is a useful technique.

Help your coachee to specify when, where and how often she will carry out the homework assignment

In this step-by-step guide, I have stressed the value of being specific as you assess your coachee's emotional problem and intervene accordingly. This principle is also useful in homework negotiation and if the assignment warrants it, then encourage your coachee to specify when, where and how often she is going to do the task. In my experience, encouraging your coachee to be specific reduces the chances that she will say that she did not do the assignment because she did not have time or the opportunity to do so.

Help your coachee to rehearse the homework assignment in the session

If you have time to do so, then encouraging your coachee to rehearse the assignment in the coaching session can be valuable. Indeed, with some assignments such rehearsal is so important that I strongly urge you to devote time to it. Rehearsal may either be mental (where your coachee pictures herself carrying out the assignment in her mind's eye) or behavioural (where your coachee role-plays with you what she has agreed to do when that involves another person). In this latter case, you may need to know a little about the other person if you are to play the role of that person in a plausible manner. I played the role of Linda's boss when she rehearsed what she was going to say to him at her planned meeting.

It is important that you encourage your coachee to practise her flexible and non-extreme attitude before and during the rehearsal.

Elicit from the coachee potential obstacles to homework completion and problem-solve these obstacles

The more you can encourage your coachee to identify potential obstacles to doing a negotiated homework assignment and help them either to circumvent such obstacles or to neutralise them, the more likely your coachee is to do the assignment. Unidentified obstacles will prevent your coachee from carrying out her homework assignment. Forewarned is forearmed for both of you.

Encourage your coachee and yourself to make and retain a written note of the homework assignment and its relevant details

Studies in medicine have shown that when the patient is given a written note by the physician of what medication to take, when and how often, this increases patient compliance with the medication routine. This is useful in coaching too and I suggest that you encourage your coachee to make a written note of the assignment and related issues (e.g. time, place and frequency). It is important that you make a written note of this too in your notes. You may want to check that you both have an accurate record of the negotiated assignment if you suspect that this may not be the case.

Having discussed important issues with respect to homework negotiation, I will discuss similar issues with respect to reviewing homework in the following step.

Case study: Negotiating homework assignments with Linda

I negotiated a number of homework assignments with Linda that I present in the order in which she did them. She saw that the purpose of all these techniques was to help her strengthen her conviction in her flexible and non-extreme attitude.

Rational-emotive imagery (REI)

I first suggested that Linda practise REI at least three times a day for ten minutes per day. She agreed to do this and we decided together that she would do it before breakfast in her bedroom, after lunch in the quiet room at work and before supper in her bedroom. She foresaw no obstacles to her doing this. I gave her a set of written instructions on how to implement the technique (Dryden, 2001).

The attack–response technique

Having taught Linda how to use the attack–response technique, I suggested that she carry out the technique in writing before our next session. She agreed to do this on Saturday afternoon at 1 pm in her bedroom. Again, Linda foresaw no obstacles to her doing this. Again I gave her a set of written instructions on how to implement the technique (Dryden, 2001).

Acting on her flexible and non-extreme attitude while rehearsing this attitude

After Linda had done the first two assignments, she agreed to talk to her boss about him breaking his promise to promote her while rehearsing her flexible and non-extreme attitude. Before she did it, we role-played the conversation with me playing her boss. Linda briefed me a little about her boss and then rehearsed her flexible and non-extreme attitude before the role-play. She was able to act on this flexible and non-extreme attitude during the role-play, after which I gave her some feedback about how she could improve her assertion skills. Again she foresaw no obstacle to doing this in reality and she had already scheduled the meeting to see her boss.

Step 19: Review homework assignments

Negotiating suitable homework assignments with your coachee shows her that such assignments are an integral part of dealing with her emotional problem. However, you can undermine this if you fail to review them at the beginning of the following session. Unless there is a very good reason not to do so (e.g. your coachee is in a state of crisis) it is good coaching practice to review the assignment at the outset of the next session and to devote sufficient time to the review to underscore its importance.

Principles in reviewing a homework assignment with your coachee

The following are a number of principles that underpin good practice in reviewing homework assignments.

When your coachee states that she did the homework assignment, check whether or not it was done as negotiated

When your coachee reports that she carried out the homework assignment, the first point to check when you review the homework assignment is whether or not she did it as negotiated. It may well be that your coachee changed the nature of the assignment and in doing so lessened the therapeutic potency of the assignment.

One common way in which your coachee may change the nature of her negotiated homework assignment is when she does not face the critical aspect of the situation that she has agreed to face. In RECBT parlance, she has not faced the 'A'. For example, let's suppose that your coachee has a fear of being rejected by a particular man. In the session you work carefully to identify, challenge and help her to change the rigid and extreme attitude that underpins her anxiety. Following on from this work, you negotiate with her an assignment that involves her practising her new flexible and non-extreme attitude in the face of actual rejection by the man. Because the coachee is afraid of rejection, it is important that she faces the prospect of rejection. At the next session, your coachee is pleased with the result of her homework. She asked the man if he wanted to go for a coffee and he accepted her invitation. However, you know that the coachee's 'A' was asking the man for a date.

As they are colleagues, they often go for a coffee and the man would not have seen it as a 'date'. The important point to note from a therapeutic point of view is that the coachee has not faced the 'A' that she agreed to face, i.e. the prospect of a date. She played safe.

How do you respond when it becomes clear that your coachee has changed the nature of her homework? I suggest that you do the following.

Step 1: Encourage your coachee by saying that you were pleased that she did the assignment.

Step 2: Explain how, in your opinion, she changed the assignment and remind her of the exact nature of the task as it was negotiated by the two of you in the previous session. In doing so, if indicated, remind your coachee of the purpose of the assignment, which dictated its precise form.

Step 3: If your coachee made a genuine mistake in changing the nature of the assignment, invite her to redo the assignment, but this time as it was previously negotiated. If she agrees, ensure that she keeps a written reminder of the assignment and ask her to guard against making further changes to it. Don't forget to review the assignment in the following session. If she doesn't agree to do the assignment, explore and deal with this reluctance.

Step 4: If it appears that the change that your coachee made to the assignment was motivated by the presence of an implicit rigid and extreme attitude, identify and deal with this attitude and again invite your coachee to redo the assignment as it was previously negotiated, urging her once again to guard against making further changes to the assignment. Alternatively, modify the assignment in a way that takes into account the newly discovered obstacle.

Review what your coachee learned from doing the assignment

It is important that you ask your coachee what she learned from doing the homework. If your coachee learned what you hoped she would learn, acknowledge that she did well and move on. If your coachee did not learn what you hoped she would learn, then you need to address this issue. In particular, help her to learn the appropriate point and see if you can help her choose another assignment that will help her learn the point experientially and not just cognitively.

Capitalise on your coachee's success

When your coachee has successfully done her homework and has learned what you hoped she would learn, reinforce her for achievement and suggest that she builds on her success by perhaps choosing a more challenging assignment next time, if appropriate.

Responding to your coachee's homework 'failure'

Let us suppose that your coachee has done her homework, but it turned out poorly. When this happens, coachees often say that they did the assignment, but 'it didn't work'. I have put the word 'failure' in inverted commas here because although coachees regard the assignment as a 'failure', there is much to learn from this situation. So, when you encounter this so-called 'failure', remind your coachee of the 'no lose' nature of homework assignments (discussed earlier) and begin to investigate the factors involved. But first ask for a factual account about what happened. Then, once you have identified the factors that accounted for the 'failure', help your coachee to deal with them and endeavour to renegotiate the same or a similar assignment. While you are investigating the factors which accounted for your coachee's homework 'failure', it is useful to keep in mind a number of such factors. Here is an illustrative list of some of the more common reasons for home-work 'failure' and possible therapeutic responses.

- **Problem:** Your coachee implemented certain but not all elements of the negotiated assignment. For example, your coachee may have done the behavioural aspect of the assignment, but did not practise new flexible and non-extreme attitudes with the result that she experienced the same UNEs associated with the target problem.

  Possible response: Suggest that she remember to rehearse her flexible and non-extreme attitudes before the behavioural part of the task. Use an in-session imagery technique, if required.

- **Problem:** The assignment was 'overwhelming rather than challenging' for your coachee at this time.

  Possible response: Encourage the coachee to see this as good feedback and recalibrate the assignment so that it is in the 'challenging' realm, not the 'overwhelming' realm.

- **Problem:** Your coachee began to do the assignment but stopped doing it because she started to experience discomfort which she believed she could not tolerate.

  Possible response: Help her to formulate an appropriate discomfort tolerance attitude and suggest that she rehearses this next time this happens.

- **Problem:** Your coachee practised the wrong flexible and non-extreme attitude during the assignment.

  Possible response: Ascertain the reason for your coachee practising the wrong attitude and suggest a suitable remedy. Suggest that she write the correct attitude on a card and take it with her to review in relevant situations.

- **Problem:** Your coachee practised the right flexible and non-extreme attitudes, but did so in an overly weak manner with the result that her UNEs predominated.

  Possible response: Suggest that she be more forceful with herself in rehearsing flexible and non-extreme attitudes. Model this in the session, if necessary.

- **Problem:** Your coachee began to do the assignment, but forgot what she was to do after she had begun.

  Possible response: Suggest that she consults a written record of the assignment in such circumstances. If she 'forgets' to do so, the obstacle needs further assessment.

- **Problem:** Your coachee began the assignment, but gave up because she did not experience immediate benefit from it.

  Possible response: Help her to see that while such immediate benefit would be nice, it is not necessary and also not likely. Help her to take a longer-range view of such benefit.

- **Problem:** Your coachee began the assignment, but gave up soon after when she realised that she did not know what to do. This happens particularly with written 'ABC' homework assignments.

Possible response: Give her a set of written instructions concerning the task (see Dryden, 2001, for examples).

- Problem: Your coachee began the assignment, but encountered another 'A' that triggered a new undiscovered rigid and extreme attitude which led her to abandon the assignment.

  Possible response: Suggest if this happens again that she look for and challenge the new rigid and extreme attitude before returning to the agreed task.

Dealing with the situation when your coachee has not done the homework assignment

Despite the fact that you may have taken the utmost care in negotiating a homework assignment with your coachee and instituted all the safeguards that I discussed above, your coachee may still not carry it out. When this happens, I suggest that you follow a similar procedure to the one previously discussed; that is, ask your coachee for a factual account of the situation where she contracted to do the assignment but did not do it, remind her of the 'no lose' concept of homework assignments, identify and deal with the factors that accounted for her not doing the assignment and then renegotiate the same or a similar assignment. As you investigate the aforementioned factors, be particularly aware of the fact that you may have failed to institute one or more of the safeguards reviewed above. If this is the case and your failure to do so accounts for your coachee not carrying out the assignment, then take responsibility for this omission, disclose this to your coachee, institute the safeguard(s) and renegotiate the assignment.

On the other hand, if the reason why your coachee did not do the assignment can be attributed to a factor in the coachee that you could not have foreseen, help her to deal with it and again renegotiate the same or a similar assignment.

Case study: Reviewing homework assignments with Linda

I reviewed each of the following assignments with Linda.

Rational-emotive imagery

Linda practised REI and reported no problems with it. I asked her to tell me how she used the technique and discovered that she used it correctly. She said that it helped her to 'feel her way' into the frame of mind of her flexible and non-extreme attitude at times when she reviewed her boss's broken promise in her mind.

The attack–response technique

Here I will present what Linda gave me and I will provide in italics the same comment that I gave her verbally in the session.

Flexible and non-extreme attitude: My boss is not bad for breaking his promise to me. He is fallible and does not have to keep his promise.

[Conviction rating of flexible and non-extreme attitude = 35%]

Attack: But bosses are supposed to keep their promises. He is my boss and therefore he absolutely should have kept his promise to me.

Response: That may hold true on the planet 'Fairness', but not on the planet 'Earth'. On Earth, people can and do sometimes break their promises. This is what happened with my boss on this occasion and sadly he acted according to what was in his mind at the time. He did not have to do what I wanted him to do. If he had to, he would have no choice but to keep his promise.

But he did have a choice and unfortunately he made the wrong choice.

Attack: But that makes him a bad person. Response: No it doesn't. It makes him fallible.

[Windy's observation: I suggested to Linda that it would have been a good idea to expand on this point and stress what fallible means and how it applies to her boss's behaviour in this episode.]

Attack: But that's a cop-out.

Response: No, it's not. It's an explanation. I am not saying that he is not responsible for breaking his promise and I am not saying that his behaviour is not bad. His behaviour was bad and he is responsible for his behaviour, but this does not mean that he is a bad person. He is a human being with many different facets and can't be defined by breaking his promise to promote me.

[Conviction rating of original flexible and non-extreme attitude = 80%]

Linda found this exercise particularly helpful in strengthening her conviction in her flexible and non-extreme attitude. She pointed to the comparison she made between the planet 'Fairness' and the planet 'Earth' as being particularly persuasive and subsequently she reported that whenever she made herself unhealthily angry thinking about the broken promise, she reminded herself that 'This is Planet Earth, not Planet Fairness; he does not have to be fair', and this helped her to feel constructively annoyed instead. This often happens when coachees use the insights from RECBT. They put it into their own language and use their own imagery and when they do so, it is particularly persuasive to them.

Acting on her flexible and non-extreme attitudes while rehearsing these attitudes

As agreed, Linda spoke to her boss about him breaking his promise to promote her. She rehearsed her flexible and non-extreme attitude beforehand and managed to think rationally about his broken promise throughout their conversation. Linda started out by checking the facts as she saw them: that he had told her that she was doing good work and that he was going to promote her, and then when the time came he didn't. Her boss agreed with these facts. Linda then told him that she was annoyed that he broke his promise and wanted to understand why. Her boss said that he was prevented from promoting her by his superior who had put a block on all promotions for financial reasons. He admitted that he was wrong not to meet with her to tell her this, but did not do so because he was scared that she might be angry with him. They resolved to discuss the issue again at Linda's next appraisal.

Linda was very pleased with how she managed herself in the meeting. She considered the work we had done on her emotional problem (as outlined in this book) to be central to the positive outcome she experienced. After the meeting she experienced a sense of closure and as a result was ready to resume her coaching work with me on the personal development objectives we had set at the outset.

Step 20: Revisit and question 'A' if necessary

In Step 8, when I discussed identifying your coachee's 'A', I urged you to encourage your coachee to assume temporarily that her 'A' (i.e. the aspect that she was most disturbed about in the situation under consideration) was true. This 'A' is her individualistic adversity. I explained that you need to do this because this is the best way for you to identify the rigid and extreme attitudes that lie at the core of your coachee's disturbed reactions at 'C' in the 'ABC' framework. If you were to question your coachee's 'A' earlier in the emotional episode under consideration because you thought it was obviously distorted, you may help your coachee to realise this and she may feel better as a result. However, she would not have gained practice at identifying, challenging and changing her rigid and extreme attitudes that according to RECBT theory lie at the core of your coachee's emotional problem. Consequently, these attitudes would remain intact and would be triggered the next time she reviews examples of her problem in her mind or encounters the same 'A' in related situations.

In addition, because your coachee's disturbed feelings stem largely from her rigid and extreme attitude towards 'A' rather than from 'A' itself, your attempts to help your coachee to question this 'A' while she holds a rigid and extreme attitude towards it will be coloured by this attitude, and any reconsideration of the distorted inference she may have made at 'A' will probably be short-lived. Alternatively, once she has made progress at changing her rigid and extreme attitude towards 'A', she is more likely to be in a more objective frame of mind and it is this frame of mind that best facilitates her questioning of 'A'.

You may not need to help your coachee to question 'A' if it is clear that she is not distorted when saying that it represents an individualistic adversity. Thus, when Linda claims that her boss broke his promise to promote her, she provided evidence that supported this inference. As such, there is no point in revisiting 'A'. You only need to revisit 'A' when it seems as if it may be distorted and your coachee has not corrected the distorted inference herself after Step 17, which is when I suggest that you revisit and question 'A' if you need to.

Case study: Linda

Linda and I did not have to do any work here because it was clear that her adversity at 'A', namely 'My boss broke his promise to promote me', was true. Her boss even admitted this at their meeting.

How to question 'A'

So how do you go about helping your coachee to question 'A'? By going back to it and asking her whether or not this was the most realistic way of looking at the situation. This does not mean that she can know for certain that her 'A' was true or false for there is rarely any absolute and agreed correct way of viewing an event. What it does mean is that your coachee can weigh up all the evidence that is available to her about the situation at hand and make what is likely to be the 'best bet' about what happened.

I now list a number of ways that you can help your coachee question 'A' so that she can determine whether or not it was the most realistic way of viewing what happened in the situation in which she disturbed herself. In doing so I will show how I helped Harriet, another one of my coachees, question her 'A', after she made progress developing her flexible and non-extreme attitude towards this 'A'. Harriet's 'A' was that she thought that she was about to be sacked from her job because her boss was critical of a report that she had written. She was very anxious about this at 'C' and could not concentrate on the personal development objectives she had set in coaching. As I said, she had made good strides at dealing with her anxiety after I had encouraged her to assume that she was about to be sacked.

1. Encourage your coachee to go back to her 'ABC' and focus on what she wrote under the heading 'situation'. Then, ask her whether what she listed under 'A' was the most realistic way of viewing the situation given all the evidence to hand. This involves her considering the inference that she made that formed 'A', considering alternative inferences, evaluating all the possibilities and choosing the most realistic inference.

2. Harriet asked herself how likely it was that she would be sacked just after her boss had been critical of her report. In formulating an answer to this question, Harriet considered the following.

   a) Has my boss been critical of the work of others and they have not been subsequently fired from their job?

   Answer: Yes. My boss has very exacting standards and he is critical of people's work when they have not met those standards. But, in the last year only one person has been fired for poor work and this was only after he received verbal and written warnings about the quality of his work.

   b) Have I received any such warnings?

   Answer: No.

   c) What has been the reaction of my boss to my other work?

   Answer: It has generally been good. This is the first time he has criticised my work. Before he has said that I have done a good job or he has said nothing at all.

3. Harriet identified alternative explanations for and implications of her boss's criticism and came up with the following.

   a) My report was not up to standard and my boss was correct to criticise me, but he was not going to fire me or issue any warning.

   b) My report was not up to standard and my boss was correct to criticise me and he was not going to fire me, but he would issue a verbal warning.

   c) My report was up to standard, but my boss criticised it because he was in a bad mood about something else.

4. Finally, Harriet reviewed the evidence concerning the likelihood of these alternative explanations. In doing so,

she took into account what she knew about her boss (i.e. he was not a man to allow his moods to colour his feedback to staff) and the level of her own work. After she answered her own questions and reviewed the other alternative explanations for her boss's behaviour, Harriet concluded, based on the evidence at hand, that her report was not up to standard, but that her boss would neither fire her nor issue a verbal warning to her.

5. However, what if Harriet's boss had indicated before that he was unhappy with Harriet's work and had issued both a verbal and a written warning to her about the quality of her work? If this was the case when Harriet came to question her 'A', she would be likely to decide that her 'A' was the best bet of all the inferences she had identified (i.e. the fact that her boss criticised her work meant that she was about to be fired). However, it could still have turned out that her boss would not have fired her. Consequently, it is important to keep in mind that even your coachee's best bet at 'A' may prove to be wrong.

Other questions that you can ask your coachee about 'A' are as follows:

- How likely is it that 'A' happened (or might happen)?
- Would an objective jury agree that 'A' happened or might happen? If not, what would the jury's verdict be?
- Did you view (are you viewing) the situation realistically? If not, how could you have viewed (can you view) it more realistically?
- If you asked someone whom you could trust to give you an objective opinion about the truth or falsity of your inference about the situation at hand, what would the

person say to you and why? How would this person encourage you to view the situation instead?

- If a friend had told you that they had faced (were facing or were about to face) the same situation as you faced and had made the same inference, what would you say to him/her about the validity of their inference and why? How would you encourage the person to view the situation instead?

Note

1 Strictly speaking, you do know this on theoretical grounds, but the coachee doesn't.

Part 4

Epilogue

I hope you can see how the work I did with Linda on her emotional problem was consistent with the step-by-step guide that I discussed in Part 3 of this book. The work I did with Linda spanned three sessions, with the bulk of the work being done in two sessions and our review of her meeting with her boss and the resultant decision to resume our work on her personal development objectives taking place in the third session.

Before closing, I want to make a few general observations about the work that I did with Linda and about the step-by-step guide that I have discussed and illustrated in this book

How many sessions?

I am often asked the question concerning how many sessions one should devote to helping a coachee deal with an emotional problem before resuming more traditional coaching work. There is, actually, no simple answer to this question. As my good friend and colleague Dr. Arnold Lazarus would say, 'It depends' (Dryden, 1991). I would say that it depends on the following factors.

The complexity of the emotional problem

In general, the more complex a coachee's emotional problem, the more sessions you will need to devote to helping your coachee address it effectively.

The coachee's receptivity to RECBT

In general, the less receptive your coachee is to RECBT, the more sessions you will need to deal with your coachee's doubts, reservations and objections to the RECBT model. Of course, if it turns out that this model does not make sense to your coachee or that she cannot or does not want to use it to address her emotional problem, then you will need to refer her to someone who can help her to address the problem before returning to you for more traditional coaching work.

The skill level of the coach in using the RECBT model

In general, the less developed your RECBT skills, the more sessions you will need to devote to helping your coachee address her emotional problem. I have been using RECBT for over 30 years and, without wanting to sound immodest, I have a high level of skill in using it to help coachees address their emotional problems within both a coaching context and a counselling or psychotherapy context. Thus, you should not expect to deal with your coachees' specific emotional problems within a coaching context as quickly as I did with Linda's emotional problem until you have developed your skills in using RECBT. How do you do this? Initially by attending courses in RECBT and then by getting supervision of your work from an RECBT supervisor. I am happy to respond by email (windy@windydryden.com) to requests for relevant information on training and supervision.

Using the step-by-step model: a reminder

I want to reiterate a point that I made earlier in the book concerning the use of the step-by-step guide that I presented and illustrated in Part 3 of the book. There are advantages and disadvantages of such a guide.

Advantages of the step-by-step guide

The main advantage of the step-by-step guide is that it provides those new to RECBT with a breakdown of the steps needed to practise RECBT well when dealing with your coachees' emotional problems within a coaching context. If such a guide were not available, then you may very well struggle unduly when you come to practise RECBT. Indeed, it was in response to trainees' requests for such a guide for use in counselling and psychotherapy that I developed it in the first place (see Dryden, DiGiuseppe & Neenan, 2010) and which I have now adapted for use when dealing with coachees' emotional problems within a coaching context.

Some may argue that it is too lengthy and that there should be a guide with fewer steps for beginners. I have some sympathy with this view and, indeed, my counselling and coaching colleague Michael Neenan and I have written such a guide for trainee counsellors (Neenan & Dryden, 2006).

The reason that I prefer the longer version presented in this book is that it is easy for trainees to miss steps that the shorter guide omits and that are important to take in the practice of RECBT with certain coachees. Indeed, when I have used the shorter guide and have given feedback to a trainee that he or she has missed an important step that does not appear in the shorter guide, their response has been, not unreasonably, that the step should have been included in the guide. So, my preference is to include all the relevant steps, as I have done in this book, and to stress that you may not need to employ them all with all of your coachees. I would rather be over-inclusive and include steps that you may not need to use on every occasion than be under-inclusive and omit steps that you may need to use on some occasions, but that you can't use because you don't know about them. This is a personal view and I recognise the validity of the argument, favoured by Michael Neenan (see Neenan & Dryden, 2006), that a shorter guide is less confusing for trainees.

Disadvantages of the step-by-step guide

The main disadvantage of a step-by-step guide such as the one presented in this book is that it may stunt creativity if you follow it slavishly. Thus, there are some people who value such a guide not because it outlines a model of practice, but because in their mind it tells them exactly what to do and they think that they need to follow the steps in the precise order in which they are presented in every case with every coachee. This is not how to use the guide.

While I appreciate that as a beginner to RECBT it is comfortable using a guide such as the one I outlined in Part 3 of this book, you should only use it in this way until you have developed some competence in applying RECBT. Then, it is important that you use the steps flexibly and begin to improvise. As I said earlier in the book, the steps are like chords and scales. You need to become proficient in their use before you improvise. Having said that, creative coaching depends on the creative implementation of techniques and strategies that are tailored for use with individual coachees rather than following a 'one size fits all' approach. This point applies whether you are working to help your coachee overcome the obstacle of her emotional problem or reach her personal development objectives.

So learn your scales, but then improvise! On that note, we have reached the end of the book.

References

Beck, A. T. (1976). *Cognitive therapy and the emotional disorders.* New York: International Universities Press.

Bordin, E. S. (1979). The generalizability of the psychoanalytic concept of the working alliance. *Psychotherapy: Theory, Research and Practice, 16(3)*, 252–260.

Cavanagh, M. J. (2005). Mental-health issues and challenging clients in executive coaching. In M. J. Cavanagh, A. M. Grant, & T. Kemp (Eds.), *Evidence-based coaching: Theory, research and practice from the behavioural sciences* (pp. 21–36). Bowen Hills, QLD: Australian Academic Press.

Dryden, W. (1986). Language and meaning in RET. *Journal of Rational-Emotive Therapy, 4(2)*, 131–142.

Dryden, W. (1991). *A dialogue with Arnold Lazarus: 'It depends'.* Milton Keynes: Open University Press.

Dryden, W. (2001). *Reason to change: A rational emotive behaviour therapy (REBT) workbook.* Hove: Brunner-Routledge.

Dryden, W. (2009). *Understanding emotional problems: The REBT perspective.* Hove: Routledge.

Dryden, W. (2011). *Counselling in a nutshell*, 2nd edition. London: Sage.

Dryden, W. (2016). *Attitudes in rational emotive behaviour therapy: Components, characteristics and adversity-related consequences.* London: Rationality Publications.

Dryden, W. (2017). *The coaching alliance: Theory and guidelines for practice.* Abingdon, Oxon: Routledge.

Dryden, W., DiGiuseppe, R., & Neenan, M. (2010). *A primer on rational emotive behavior therapy*, 3rd edition. Champaign, IL: Research Press.

Ellis, A. (1979). Discomfort anxiety: A new cognitive behavioral construct. Part 1. *Rational Living, 14(2)*, 3–8.

Ellis, A. (1980). Discomfort anxiety: A new cognitive behavioral construct. Part 2. *Rational Living, 15(1)*, 25–30.

Ellis, A. (2005). *The myth of self-esteem*. Amherst, NY: Prometheus.

Ellis, A., & Maultsby, M. C. (1974). *Techniques for using rational-emotive imagery*. New York: Institute for Rational Living.

Neenan, M., & Dryden, W. (2006). *Rational emotive behaviour therapy in a nutshell*. London: Sage.

Index

For Product Safety Concerns and Information please contact our EU
representative GPSR@taylorandfrancis.com
Taylor & Francis Verlag GmbH, Kaufingerstraße 24, 80331 München, Germany